Stitching Your Story Piece by Peace

Stitching Your Story Piece by Peace

A 13-Week Devotional

Pursuing the Peace of God

Naomi Fata

ISBN: 979-8-9907865-0-9
ISBN: 979-8-9907865-1-6 (electronic)

Christian Resource Ministry Inc.
PO Box 448
Rhinebeck, NY 12572

In memory of my dad,
Walter C. Irwin III
1942-2018
Not a father by blood, but fully a father in spirit.
I love you. I would not be who I am today without you.

Dedicated to my sewing sisters.
May this book speak your sewing language and draw you close
to the heart of Father God.

Contents

Preface 13

How to Use This Book 14

Are you in a position to receive the peace of God? 16

Week 1: The Purpose of Sewing 19

    Day 1   20

    Day 2   23

    Day 3   25

    Day 4   27

    Day 5   29

    Day 6   31

Week 2: The History of Stitching 33

    Day 1   34

    Day 2   36

    Day 3   38

    Day 4   41

    Day 5   43

    Day 6   45

Week 3: The Power of Belief 47

    Day 1   48

    Day 2   50

    Day 3   52

    Day 4   54

    Day 5   56

    Day 6   58

Week 4: Jesus as The Teacher of Peace 61

    Day 1   62

    Day 2   64

    Day 3   66

    Day 4   68

Day 5   70

Day 6   72

Week 5: Trust Brings Peace 75

Day 1   76

Day 2   78

Day 3   80

Day 4   82

Day 5   84

Day 6   86

Week 6: All the Parts Working Together 89

Day 1   90

Day 2   92

Day 3   94

Day 4   96

Day 5   98

Day 6   100

Week 7: Tangled Threads 103

Day 1   104

Day 2   106

Day 3   108

Day 4   110

Day 5   112

Day 6   114

Week 8: Overwhelm Steals Peace 117

Day 1   118

Day 2   120

Day 3   122

Day 4   124

Day 5   126

Day 6   128

Week 9: Identity Impacts Peace 131

Day 1   132

Day 2   134

Day 3   136

Day 4   138

Day 5   140

Day 6   142

Week 10: Troubleshooting Peace 145

Day 1   146

Day 2   148

Day 3   150

Day 4   152

Day 5   154

Day 6   156

Week 11: Connection To God 159

Day 1   160

Day 2   162

Day 3   164

Day 4   166

Day 5   168

Day 6   170

Week 12: Integrated Connection 173

Day 1   174

Day 2   176

Day 3   178

Day 4   180

Day 5   182

Day 6   184

Week 13: Choose Your Stitches 187

Day 1   188

Day 2   190

Day 3   192

    Day 4   194

    Day 5   196

    Day 6   198

Epilogue 201

Acknowledgements 202

Glossary 203

Recommended Reading 204

About the Author 206

Endnotes 207

Preface

I wrote an outline for this book in 2017. After earning a diploma in Christian Life Coaching, and years of reading, and processing through my past, I thought I was reading to write on the topic of anxiety. However, God had different plans. In 2018, my spiritual father, Walt, passed away, leaving my emotions in a tailspin. He had been my pillar of encouragement for my writing life by filling the role of both father and mentor.

In the years since his passing, I tried to pick up the outline several times, but I could not make any progress. Then, in 2022, I joined the Inkwell writing community. I knew it was time to write the manuscript but didn't know where to start. One woman encouraged, "Start from where you are." This was a pivotal moment, as at the very moment she spoke those words I was sitting at my sewing machine.

Through this word of encouragement and many others, I shaped this book not as the voice of an academic or a Bible scholar, but from my perspective sitting at the sewing machine. The outcome is far more creative than I could have imagined, and I have had so much fun putting the sewing imagery into words.

How to Use This Book

Begin each day by quieting your heart.

Take a moment to reflect on your level of peace. Consider playing a worship song. Reflect on 1 Peter 5:7, "Give all your worries and cares to God, for he cares about you."

Turn this into a prayer:

Thank You, Lord, that You care for me. I give you my worries about a certain situation, trusting that You are in control. Amen.

Time

Give yourself at least 20 minutes a day. You could separate it and do the ten minutes of reading at one time and the journaling activity later in the day if you choose.

Read in Consecutive Order!

Each week builds on the previous one, as these concepts build on each other. Resist the temptation to read out of order.

Power Prayer

Second Corinthians 10:5 reminds us to take every thought captive. It is important to train your thoughts to know the truth. When a lie comes into our thinking, it is helpful to have words of truth to combat it. At the end of each day, you will notice a power prayer.

These prayers are rooted in thanksgiving because as my friend Rosemary says, "Thanksgiving is an enabling power as you activate the Word of God by inviting Him to fulfill His Word." When you are struggling with a negative thought pattern, the best thing to do is come to God with thanksgiving rooted in Scripture, which will help you build new memory pathways in your brain.

If you wish, you can close your power prayer with "Amen." I tend to think of these prayers as a continual conversation with God; therefore, I did not close them with an Amen.

A 6-Day Week

This work of processing our inner life is heavy. Rather than overwhelm you with seven days of inner work, I encourage you to take the seventh day to just spend time with the Lord. Process what you learned during the week and refresh your soul.

13 Weeks

Thirteen weeks is intentional, because it takes roughly 90 days to make a new habit part of your life. I want awareness of your inner life of peace to become a habit.

Use the Resources Available to You

This book focuses on peace versus anxiety from a spiritual lens. There are many other resources available to help with anxiety such as counseling, therapy, medical help and dietary changes. These are resources that you may also need to use.

Are you in a position to receive the peace of God?

If you do not have a personal relationship with Christ, the peace I write about in this book is not available to you. Acts 16:31 says to believe in the Lord Jesus Christ and you will be saved.

If you have not yet received the free gift of forgiveness for sin through the death, burial and resurrection of Jesus, the Son of God, don't go another day without coming to know Him.

The following was written by my spiritual dad, Walt, outlining the way of salvation.

God loves you.

"For God so loved the world that he gave his one and only Son, that whoever believes in him shall not perish but have eternal life." John 3:16

God Has a plan for you. He wants you to have a satisfying, abundant life.

"The thief comes only to steal and kill and destroy; I have come that they may have life, and have it to the full." John 10:10

Do you have a satisfying life?

Sin keeps you from experiencing God's plan for you. We have all broken God's law (the 10 commandments).

"For all have sinned and fall short of the glory of God." Romans 3:23

You are separated from God because of sin.

"For the wages of sin is death, but the gift of God is eternal life in Christ Jesus our Lord." Romans 6:23

God has an answer to this dilemma.

"But God demonstrates his own love for us in this: While we were still sinners, Christ died for us." Romans 5:8

He sent His Son Jesus who is a provision for our sin.

"For what I received I passed on to you as of first importance: that Christ died for our sins according to the Scriptures, that he was buried, that he was raised on the third day according to the Scriptures, and that he appeared to Cephas, and then to the Twelve.

After that, he appeared to more than five hundred of the brothers and sisters at the same time, most of whom are still living, though some have fallen asleep." 1 Corinthians 15:3-6

Jesus is the only way to experience eternal life.

"Jesus answered, 'I am the way and the truth and the life. No one comes to the Father except through me.'" John 14:6

It is not enough to know these things; you must receive Him.

"He came to that which was his own, but his own did not receive him. Yet to all who did receive him, to those who believed in his name, he gave the right to become children of God." John 1:11-12

All you need to do is trust Him to save you. This is true faith.

"For it is by grace you have been saved, through faith—and this is not from yourselves, it is the gift of God— not by works, so that no one can boast." Ephesians 2:8-9

He personally invites you to have a relationship with Him.

"Here I am! I stand at the door and knock. If anyone hears my voice and opens the door, I will come in and eat with that person, and they with me." Revelation 3:20

When you have a relationship with Jesus, you have eternal life.

"And this is the testimony: God has given us eternal life, and this life is in his Son. Whoever has the Son has life; whoever does not have the Son of God does not have life. I write these things to you who believe in the name of the Son of God so that you may know that you have eternal life. This is the confidence we have in approaching God: that if we ask anything according to his will, he hears us." 1 John 5:11-14

Thank God for what He has done for you.

"Thanks be to God for his indescribable gift!" 2 Corinthians 9:15

Prayer: God, I am a sinner. I am sorry for my sin. I receive Jesus as my Savior. I confess Him as my Lord. Amen.

This is also available on the Christian Resource Ministry website: https://christianresourceministry.com/what-is-salvation/

Week 1: The Purpose of Sewing

Thank You Father, for teaching me secure attachment as I become rooted and built up in Christ.

Day 1

My daughter tore off the Christmas wrapping paper to reveal a gorgeous mauve sweater with bell sleeves. She was so excited to wear it to church the next Sunday. But the excitement didn't last long. As she tried on the sweater, a stitch unraveled, only to leave the sleeve hanging wide open. Panic set in as she bemoaned her new outfit, now in pieces.

From the perspective of a sewist, I could calm her by reassuring her that stitching the seam back together would be a simple task. The problem was straightforward enough—the stitches weren't secure, causing the pieces to fall apart.

Here lies the secret. The stitches aren't secure. The principle of sewing is simple. It is cloth stitched together to create something exquisite, whether a work of art, an article of clothing or some other textile.

Just think of all the work required to construct a beautiful garment, only to have it fall apart because the stitches are loose. In the same way, how often do we spend our lives in church, in Bible study, and reading Christian literature, but never examine the stitches? As we do the "Christian" thing, are the truths that we are learning to become entwined in our lives, holding together the moments of our days? The assumption is that knowing the Christian lingo, the good theology and acting the part should always end with the perfect church girl outcome, right?

This morning I listened to an interview on Grace Enough Podcast with my friend Leigh Mackenzie as she spoke about her book, "She Seems So Normal: Shatter the Plastic Princess, Embrace Authentic Faith." After she came to faith in Christ, she did all the right things and became known as a church leader along with her husband, yet she realized that the fruit of the spirit was not visible in her life. This was because of unresolved trauma from the past. Until she examined the "stitches" of her childhood—literally the things that were sewn into her as a child—she was just covering it over with the plastic face of a church girl.[1]

The goal of sewing is to join fabric together securely. But if the very stitches are unstable, unhealthy, or brittle, the sewing will not be very secure. In the same manner, the goal of our Christian faith is to join our soul to the Father so that He may live through us, shape us, comfort us, and dwell within us. In my experience, I know that doing all the right things does not mean our relationship with Father God feels rich and secure. Childhood attachment, which was formed by my family and circumstances, shaped much of my connection to God. This is true of us all. The past shapes us. It gives us a schema through which we interact with the world.

Having faith in Christ and reading the Bible doesn't instantly alter our pre-existing schemas.

Read Colossians 2:6-7, "So then, just as you received Christ Jesus as Lord, continue to live your lives in him, rooted and built up in him, strengthened in the faith as you were taught, and overflowing with thankfulness."

John 15:5, "I am the vine; you are the branches. If you remain in me and I in you, you will bear much fruit; apart from me, you can do nothing."

Reflect on your connection with God as Your Father. Circle the words below that describe how you feel about the relationship.

Supported

Fearful

Distant

Confident

Judged

Loved

Safe

Restful

Striving to Please

Driven

What are your thoughts about the goal of your Christian faith having a secure attachment to God as your Father?

Record Your Thoughts

Prayer: Father, I believe that You want me to be rooted and built in You, as a secure stitch holding me to Yourself. Help me to recognize any areas of insecure attachment to You as my Father. Thank You for being the Father I can trust, Who is LOVE and never fails. Give me the ability to trust You securely, even when I don't feel that I am able. Amen.

Power Prayer for Week 1: Thank You, Father, for teaching me secure attachment as I become rooted and built up in Christ.

Day 2

In recent years, as I started teaching sewing, I've also started reading more about the fast fashion industry. A frequent question I get asked is about the quality of fabrics in relation to why our clothes do not last as long as they used to. While fabric quality is part of the issue, compromised stitches are an even more significant reason clothing is not being held together. In her book "Overdressed: The Shockingly High Cost of Cheap Fashion," Elizabeth Cline interviewed designer Eliza Starbuck about the fashion industry. Starbuck discussed how production compromises sewing for the sake of speed and costs, explaining that factories may use a looser, less-secure stitch to expedite garment production.[2]

In this example of fast fashion, some issues have nothing to do with the fabric and everything to do with the stitching. In a similar way, I think that we often blame anxiety and lack of peace on a genetic disposition, when it may be completely unrelated to genetics. John Hopkins Medical School conducted a 30-year study to research if "a single related cause existed for mental illness, hypertension, malignant tumors, coronary heart disease and suicide."[3] Surprisingly, the predicator of these maladies has nothing to do with genetics, but the key factor was lack of closeness to the parents, particularly the father.

This story was an integral part of my childhood. The memories of my father's illness are vague. But I remember the last visit to the hospital. It was evening, and a snowstorm was coming. My brother, mother and I said good night and drove home. The next morning, I woke up to my mom sitting on the piano bench in the living room. All I remember were the words, "He's gone." At that moment, I didn't have overwhelming feelings of grief. I took it in as a fact of life—death comes to all of us. My focus was on the fact that he was in heaven.

What I didn't know then was that losing him shaped my childhood and my attachment. My seven-year-old self had no words for abandonment. Yet, losing a parent affected my ability to attach securely to God. As Tim Clinton and Joshua Straub relate in the book "God Attachment," how we attach to our parents correlates to how we attach to God as our Father. Without a secure attachment to God, it is only natural that we have a hard time handling the stress of life, which leads to such things as that mental illness, hypertension, etc. as proven by the John Hopkins study.

Read: Psalm 56:8, "Record my misery; list my tears on your scroll— are they not in your record?

Prayer: before beginning this exercise: Father, thank You for being there in my childhood. I know you saw what I experienced. I believe Your Word that says, "You kept track of all my pain" (Psalm 56:8). As I reflect on my past, may Your presence with me now be a source of comfort and healing. Thank You for the gift of Your Spirit, who is my comfort. Amen.

Reflect: Use the lines below to journal some reflections of your childhood. Did you feel close to your parents? Write specific memories that may be painful to you. Write whatever comes to mind; both what was good and what was painful.

How does it make you feel to know that God kept track of all your pain?

Record Your Thoughts

Prayer: Father, though my past was painful, I believe You were there with me. Thank You for not forsaking me. Give me the eyes to see all the times when You were there beside me, delivering me even in times of great pain. Amen.

Power Prayer for Week 1: Thank You, Father, for teaching me secure attachment as I become rooted and built up in Christ.

Day 3

The voice on the other end of the phone had that high-pitched, anxious strain, "I tried on my dress to see how it would look with my jewelry, and as I was moving around, I heard beads dropping on the floor. I'm so afraid that the beads are all going to come off, and I don't even know where they are coming from. I just don't understand. I picked up my dress from the bridal shop only yesterday and it was totally fine when I tried it on there."

Calmly, I reassured this bride that it is all fixable. The dress manufacturer often stitches on the bead work by machine. On the rack, or the mannequin, dresses appear to be perfect, but when one thread catches it can cause an entire row of beads to fall on the floor. I asked her to check for an extra package of beads that typically come with formal gowns and promised her she will look perfect on her special day, and no one will know this mishap ever occurred.

Without secure attachment, beads fall off, but this situation is repairable. In life, without secure parental attachment during our formative years, as we enter adulthood and experience more "pressure" in life, the unraveling may begin.

As I progressed in my motherhood journey, I unraveled. Underneath the surface, I could feel the dark clouds of anxiety, overwhelm, and anger swirling. I battled the storm through study, reading books by counselors, psychologists, and neuroscientist Dr. Caroline Leaf. I learned about the four basic attachment styles in attachment theory. Anxious attachment is an insecure attachment to the parental figure, or a neediness. Avoidant attachment is a fear of intimacy, keeping others at arm's length. Fearful-avoidant attachment could stem from abuse, where the child is fearful of the parent. Last, there is secure attachment, which is the goal.

In my first book, "Beyond Head Knowledge," I wrote how while I was growing up in the church, God still felt distant. His promises did not seem like the ever-present reality that was written in Scripture. When I wrote that book, I had no education on attachment theories. As I investigated my childhood, I saw how my attachment to God was between the three unhealthy attachment types, primarily avoidant attachment and fearful-avoidant. I kept God at arm's length, attempting to please Him with my good works. Experiencing the death of my father at a young age caused me to fear abandonment from other parental figures, such as God. As I processed the emotions of my past, and grew in my understanding of Father God, I began to form secure attachment.

Read: Isaiah 41:10, "So do not fear, for I am with you; do not be dismayed, for I am your God; I will strengthen you and help you; I will uphold you with my righteous right hand."
Isaiah 61:1, "The Spirit of the Sovereign Lᴏʀᴅ is on me, because the Lᴏʀᴅ has anointed me, to proclaim good news to the poor. He has sent me to bind up the brokenhearted, to proclaim freedom for the captives and release from darkness for the prisoners."

Reflect: What is your relationship with your spouse, parents, siblings, or close friends? Which of the four attachment types do you think you model?

Record Your Thoughts

Prayer: Father, I need you to show me the love of the Father that was not modeled to me in childhood. I want so badly to attach to you securely. Help me. Fill me. Heal me. Thank you for your promise to heal my broken heart. Amen.

Power Prayer for Week 1: Thank You, Father, for teaching me secure attachment as I become rooted and built up in Christ.

Day 4

I could see the fabric in my mind's eye. I thought I had just enough to make a black circle skirt. We didn't shop for new clothes much because of financial constraints. Between that and being in that awkward stage of adolescence, halfway between girl child and woman, I was self-conscious about my clothing and always dreaming of ways to make new things. I was convinced a new outfit would solve all my problems.

The preacher jarred me from my daydreaming as he directed us to stand for the closing hymn of another Sunday service. In church, I day-dreamed about fabric, but every night I went to bed dreaming of what it would be like to have a father again. I thought that if my mother remarried, it would cure me of all my pain. But no amount of hoping or praying brought this dream to pass.

By the time I was 17, I buried the dreams of my father and faced the reality of earning my way in the world by working at the local convenience store to contribute to the family income. One day during those first years at the convenience store, a middle-aged locksmith came into the store. On seeing my name tag "Naomi," he began a conversation about the root of my name being from the Bible. Through this he found out that I was a believer. This was the beginning of one of the greatest miracles of my life. I didn't get a father in the picturesque way that I had dreamed of through a fairy tale remarriage of my mom. Instead, a father came to me when I was working at the lowest of jobs—flipping eggs, making coffee, and cleaning the public restroom of a gas station. In fact, it was close to ten years later before God revealed to me that this locksmith was the father figure for whom I had always prayed. Over the course of the years, I formed a secure attachment with this locksmith named Walt.

As you read this story of my miracle father, and the healing journey that followed, I pray you do not think that something like this couldn't happen to you. Instead, may this story cause hope to rise in you. God showed up when I least expected, and this was when I was angry about my lot in life.

Often God has the answers to our prayers and the healing that we need right in front of us, but sometimes we must be brave enough to see it, let someone into our pain to heal us, and trust God to rewrite our story. As we lean into Christ, He gives the courage so we can form secure attachments that will heal our stories.

Read: Jeremiah 29:11, "For I know the plans I have for you," declares the LORD, "plans to prosper you and not to harm you, plans to give you hope and a future."

Reflect: What is it you feel you need to heal your story? There is no correct answer, but the naming of things brings it forward into our awareness. This may be something that you've daydreamed about before or are daydreaming about now.

Record Your Thoughts

Prayer: Thank You, Father for all that you have given me. Father, I know you created me with mind, will, and emotions. I think that having (a certain situation) would help heal my heart. I believe that You have a good plan for me, and I believe that part of that plan will happen as I connect with Your people. Show me the people that you have put in my life as safe spaces. Amen.

Power Prayer for Week 1: Thank You, Father, for teaching me secure attachment as I become rooted and built up in Christ.

Day 5

I carried the embroidered chiffon to the cutting counter. It was for the bodice of my wedding gown. Finally, my life was looking up. This wedding gown was the physical representation of childhood dreams, as I wed into "happily ever after."

Before my marriage, I had developed a much deeper relationship with God, as I shared in my book "Beyond Head Knowledge." I thought that several spiritual experiences in the year before our marriage had healed me from my past. But by the time I was pregnant with my second child, I realized that my childhood issues were resurfacing. I knew God; I believed in Him and trusted Him, yet I had overwhelming bouts of fear and anger. The responsibility of raising a crying, needy toddler left me undone. I read parenting books on properly disciplining children and creating a peaceful home, yet a war still raged within my heart and mind.

I had come so far in recognizing the roots of the evil one, the importance of abiding, and hearing the voice of God as my Father, yet I still struggled. After publishing my first book, I realized that I still had a long way to go. I began taking life coaching classes, and reading Christian authors who focused on the mind and soul development. Though I didn't know where the journey would take me, I knew I needed to be whole if not for my sake, for the sake of my own children. I knew enough to understand that if I lived with issues of fear and anger, I would pass them down to my descendants, as we all learn by example. Though God is sovereign and can change and transform everyone, children are affected by their environment.

I set out on a journey to understand myself, my reactions, my thinking patterns, and my emotions. I needed to understand my past. With all that was within me, I wanted to fight for the spiritual, emotional, and mental health of my own children, and I knew that the only way that I could do this was by changing myself. This devotional is an invitation for you to join me on your own journey.

Read: Psalm 4:8, "In peace I will lie down and sleep, for you alone, O Lord, will keep me safe."

Reflect: Observe your emotions throughout the day. Do you lie down in peace? Do you notice bouts of anger, fear, or frustration? Journal about some of these emotions and reflect on how or when they occur.

Record Your Thoughts

Prayer: Father, I struggle with (name the emotions). I don't always know why I respond this way, or where these emotions originate. Thank You for creating me with emotions. Help me learn to recognize and cultivate healthy emotions. Amen.

Power Prayer for Week 1: Thank You, Father, for teaching me secure attachment as I become rooted and built up in Christ.

Day 6

With lightning speed, I stitched around the cushion cover, ready to be done with the job. As I turned the fabric over to trim my thread ends, I saw that the loops of the top thread hung below the seam. With one tug, I could pull the bobbin thread from the entire seam. The tension was off, leaving the stitches loose and my work falling apart.

Tension is not always the first place new sewists check when starting a new seam. In the same way, attachment was not the first place I would have thought to consider in my quest for wholeness. Yet it was central to the beginning of my journey.

One of my best friends adopted two small children from Ethiopia. Before the adoption, she and her husband knew that orphaned children often have a challenging time attaching to parents. This is in part because they have not had two primary caregivers; instead, they have had many. Until now, the children had not had parents to whom they belonged, so they viewed everyone as a potential "caregivers." After the children arrived, they frequently practiced baby wearing in order to help the children bond. They primarily dedicated that first year to forming that secure attachment.

In a sense, I had a different experience with attachment. One of my caregivers had died. This gave way to feelings of abandonment. Every child may respond to abandonment differently, but my unconscious response was self-sufficiency. I had the expectation that those who were supposed to be responsible would let me down, so I felt I might as well do it myself. This type of self-sufficiency also cuts off vulnerability to protect my heart from future hurt.

These internal responses are not abnormal in a child who has lost a parent. Yet I had never been aware of how they affected my view of the world, my ability to connect with God, and my relationships with my husband, children, and friends.

The church and my knowledge of Christianity mainly emphasized salvation for the soul. That belief in Christ will save you from hell. In my church experience, too often the next steps include learning doctrine and the moral way to live according to the Bible. Yet, I question how much of discipleship focuses on starting with a secure attachment to God as our Father.

Attachment is the lens through which we view the world, our faith, and our lives. As I formed that secure attachment to Walt, my God-given dad, I worked through issues of identity, insecurity, and self-worth. To hold my faith, life, and family together, I had to learn how to stitch securely. I learned to embrace the closeness and vulnerability that occurs when I tighten that thread, which connects me to Father God and to those I love.

Read: Psalm 100:3, "Know that the Lord is God. It is he who made us, and we are his; we are his people, the sheep of his pasture."

Reflect: Do you feel you belong? In your family? In your home? In your faith? Do you believe and sense that you are God's beloved child?

Record Your Thoughts

Prayer: Father, thank You for creating me. Thank You for choosing me. I don't always feel like I belong to You, but I want to feel this way. Help me hold on to the words of Scripture that tell me I am Yours. Plant this truth deep in my heart. Amen.

Power Prayer for Week 1: Thank You, Father, for teaching me secure attachment as I become rooted and built up in Christ.

Week 2: The History of Stitching

Thank You, Father, for making a way for me to have peace.

Day 1

"I just don't have a gift for sewing."

"My grandmother sewed, but I didn't inherit her talent."

These are the statements I hear all the time. Pause for a moment. Think about the TV series "Little House on the Prairie" or "The Waltons." "Little House on the Prairie" showcased the everyday life of a pioneer family in the late 19th century while "The Waltons" took place in the Great Depression of the 1930s. The women of these families sewed. Mrs. Ingalls from "Little House on the Prairie" predominantly sewed the family's clothing because store-made clothing was still expensive before the full effects of the Industrial Revolution.

The women of the Walton family mended, repaired, quilted, and made slipcovers. Sewing was a part of their lives. It wasn't something they could choose whether to do. These women learned to sew as a skill passed on from their mothers and grandmothers before them. During that era, society expected women to learn to sew. There was no choice about whether they were "gifted in sewing."

History is often a window into the past from which we can learn. Have you ever thought about the history of peace found in the Bible? Adam and Eve enjoyed peace with God when they walked with Him in the garden. But when they ate the fruit of the tree of the knowledge of good and evil, it was then that stress and anxiety entered their lives. Previously they had not been worried about things like clothing, but after the fall it became a concern.

Can I let you in on a little secret? I didn't start off as a talented seamstress. I remember the first quilt I made as a 12-year-old. The squares weren't straight, and the seam allowance was off. I did the best I could, but it was far from "good." In your own sewing abilities, if you say you do not have them, I dare say it has more to do with not being taught and not having the self-discipline to learn than it is an inability to perform the task.

The same is true for a peaceful heart.

Too many times I have heard the flippant comments in my mom circles about how "I'm anxious and I can't help it." Or, "I'm not sleeping because I am stressed." Most always there is a resignation that anxiety is commonplace, and stress filling our lives is normal. Maybe we blame the season of parenting we are going through, the evils of technology, our own wiring, and so much more.

Rather than accepting your state of anxiety as an unchangeable fact of life, come to God knowing that He desires to teach you how to turn your anxieties over to Him. Don't belittle yourself for feeling the stress, but recognize this will be a growth journey for the rest of your life. I'm here to invite you to take the first steps.

Read: John 14:27, "Peace I leave with you; my peace I give you. I do not give to you as the world gives. Do not let your hearts be troubled and do not be afraid."

Reflect: Interact with these questions and journal your thoughts.

Is it true that some people have a natural gravitation towards sewing? Yes. Is it also true that some people have a more peaceful personality?

Do I believe everyone could learn to sew (not necessarily at a professional level but with proficiency)? Yes. Do you believe that everyone who is in Christ can live with the peace of God dwelling in them?

Record Your Thoughts

Prayer: Thank you, Father, that your peace is available to me. I struggle to have peace within, and many times find myself anxious and fearful. Help me lean into You for my peace. Amen.

Power Prayer for Week 2: Thank You, Father, for making a way for me to have peace.

Day 2

Past generations of women learned to sew for a purpose. They had to extend the life of their clothing and textiles for several reasons. Factory-made clothing was expensive and most working-class families did not have the means to hire a personal tailor or to purchase pre-made clothing. Sewing was hardly optional. Instead, knowing how to sew was a necessity for everyday life.

Like working-class families viewed pre-made clothing in the past, we perceive peace as a luxury . We believe peace is something outside our reach rather than something about which we can learn.

We think of the verses in Philippians 2:12 where Paul exhorts us to work out our salvation. Henry Morris' study Bible comments on this, saying, "We are not told to work for our salvation, but to work it out in practice in our lives."[4]

I used to think that as Christians, we either had peace or we didn't. I know it is a fruit of the spirit, so I truly wanted to have peace. Every time I felt anxious, worried, or restless (lacking peace in any way—which was ALL the time) I condemned myself with accusing words. I thought I needed to pray more, immerse myself in more Scripture, and just be a better Christian to attain peace.

Working out my peace seemed like an exceptionally hard task that didn't seem to have a path to get there. If you have never threaded a needle to sew on a button, hemming a pair of pants can feel like an insurmountable task. The learning gap between you and women of the last century seems impossible to bridge. But they were all inexperienced sewists at one time during their childhood. They simply had teachers and years of practice, which turned them into expert household sewists.

As you work out the peace of God in your heart, God does not expect you to bridge the learning gap in a matter of moments or days. He is inviting you to begin the lifelong journey of working with Him to grow in peace.

Like those women of old who sewed out of necessity to maintain a better quality of life through home-sewn mending and repair, you can also pursue peace out of necessity. Learning the path to peace will ultimately give you a better quality of life within your own soul.

Read: Philippians 2:12-18, "Therefore, my dear friends, as you have always obeyed—not only in my presence, but now much more in my absence—continue to work out your salvation with fear and trembling, for it is God who works in you to will and to act in order to fulfill his good purpose. Do everything without grumbling or arguing, so that you may become blameless and pure, "children of God without fault in a warped and crooked generation." Then you will shine among them like stars in the sky as you hold firmly to the word of life. And then I will be able to boast on the day of Christ that I did not run or labor in vain. But even if I am being poured out like a drink offering on the sacrifice and service coming from your faith, I am glad and rejoice with all of you. So you too should be glad and rejoice with me."

Reflect: What do you think it means to work out your salvation? Take some time to study and pray over this passage. Consider God's long-term plan for you, which is to enjoy fellowship with Him. How does this relate to your peace? Do you enjoy the company of someone else when you are not at peace?

Record Your Thoughts

Prayer: Father, I am overwhelmed by Your goodness. It seems almost more than I can take in—that You would desire to have me enjoy Your presence, just for the sake of being with You. I long to be at peace with You. Amen.

Power Prayer for Week 2: Thank You, Father, for making a way for me to have peace.

Day 3

Did you know that sewing is the first recorded invention of man in the Bible? In Genesis 3:7, Adam and Eve knew they were naked and sewed fig leaves to cover themselves.

Now that we are back at the beginning of the Bible, think about the relationship Adam and Eve had with God before they needed to sew their clothes. They were at peace. It was a relationship without shame, guilt, hiding, or condemnation. Because the world seems big and complicated, and because we are so far removed from God's original design of continually peaceful fellowship with Him, we can truly overcomplicate peace.

I perceive peace as the absence of conflict, or tranquility. It involves a sort of harmony within our souls. Our souls have harmony with God because we trust Him completely. That trust got all messed up when Adam and Eve first ate the forbidden fruit. Suddenly, we could be like God. We could rationalize, fear, and control future outcomes. The focus of life was no longer on resting in the perfect relationship with God as Father and friend. Instead, it turned to self-preservation.

God loved you so much that he provided a path for peace to be made. In the Old Testament, peace offerings established this path. The first several books of the Bible record the accounts of Noah, Abraham, Isaac, Jacob, and Joseph, who followed God but who also had struggled with their own sinful condition. If you read their accounts, you will see records of drunkenness, lying, sexual immorality, and incest among them. Yet, God used them.

Rather than leave them hopeless, God set protocol in place for how His people could approach Him. The book of Leviticus records a variety of offerings that God instituted as a means for His people to restore a relationship with Him. I remember reading about these offerings the first time I read the Bible cover to cover as a zealous teenager. But I had never truly noticed the peace offering mentioned in Leviticus 7.

The purpose of all Old Testament offerings was to transfer the guilt of a sinner onto a perfect animal through the shedding of blood. These sacrifices were to allow us a relationship with our Holy Father, which gives us peace with God. Each type of sacrifice had significance. "The idea of thanksgiving was associated with the peace offering." It was "brought in response to an unexpected blessing or an answer to prayer, or for general thankfulness."[5]

This peace offering represented our fellowship upward to God — the ability of our hearts to have peace with Him through the offering of thanksgiving. Knowing that God Himself is the one who planned the peace offering in the first place is a poignant reminder that God's plan is peace. He did not leave us to face this world alone and carrying the weight of stress. He made a clear path to peace.

Read: Leviticus 7:11-18, "'These are the regulations for the fellowship offering anyone may present to the Lord:

'If they offer it as an expression of thankfulness, then along with this thank offering they are to offer thick loaves made without yeast and with olive oil mixed in, thin loaves made without yeast and brushed with oil, and thick loaves of the finest flour well-kneaded and with oil mixed in. Along with their fellowship offering of thanksgiving they are to present an offering with thick loaves of bread made with yeast. They are to bring one of each kind as an offering, a contribution to the Lord; it belongs to the priest who splashes the blood of the fellowship offering against the altar. The meat of their fellowship offering of thanksgiving must be eaten on the day it is offered; they must leave none of it till morning.

"'If, however, their offering is the result of a vow or is a freewill offering, the sacrifice shall be eaten on the day they offer it, but anything left over may be eaten on the next day. Any meat of the sacrifice left over till the third day must be burned up. If any meat of the fellowship offering is eaten on the third day, the one who offered it will not be accepted. It will not be reckoned to their credit, for it has become impure; the person who eats any of it will be held responsible.'"

Psalm 116:17, "I will sacrifice a thank offering to you and call on the name of the Lord."

Reflect: Reading through the book of Leviticus with all the sacrifices and rules can be hard to understand. Ask God to help clear your mind and heart to show you His heart and your peace. What are some things for which you are thankful? How can you offer those to God as a peace offering?

Record Your Thoughts

Prayer: Father, thank You for Your plan for peace. I thank You for making a way for the Old Testament saints to experience peace, and I thank You for the gift of Jesus as my path to peace today. I ask that through the Holy Spirit, you would show me to live at peace. Amen.

Power Prayer for Week 2: Thank You, Father, for making a way for me to have peace.

Day 4

I wonder what Adam and Eve used to sew their fig leaves together. Since they didn't eat animals, they may not have carved their needle from a bone. Perhaps they carved it from a twig. It's pure speculation, but I am certain that I have never used the method that they used.

Times change. Now I predominately use the sewing machine.

Wood and bone are no longer the typical method for sewing. The peace offering described in the Old Testament is no longer the required method to access the peace of God. Instead, God sent His only Son, the Prince of Peace (Isaiah 9:6).

Jesus became the peace offering for us through His death on the cross, so that we would have peace with God. When we come to Jesus, we now have access to complete and unreserved fellowship with God. Though the sacrifice has taken place and peace is available for our taking, we rarely seek to fully experience the peace through Jesus.

Years of broken human relationships don't give us a complete picture of what it would look like to be fully at peace in someone else's presence. I remember that just below my level of consciousness, I would wonder what I should say, how I should say it, or whether I should say everything I was thinking when talking to a loved one. There is such a thing as wisdom (knowing what to say when), but being self-conscious in all our relationships is an entirely separate thing. It takes a lot of work to learn to be confident in who Christ says that we are. That confidence first starts with knowing Him, which is possible through the peace offering He gave as the gift of Himself.

As I began to learn from my heart how deeply He loved me and how good a Father He is, I gained an inner confidence I had not previously possessed. My relationship with Christ and His work in my life was no longer confined to hope of heaven, but I realized peace with Him meant that I could exchange my broken self-esteem for His. I didn't need to feel insecure and unworthy in His presence because He says that I am loved and chosen.

Read: Isaiah 9:6, "For to us a child is born, to us a son is given, and the government will be on his shoulders. And he will be called Wonderful Counselor, Mighty God, Everlasting Father, Prince of Peace."

NOTE: If you are unfamiliar with the account of Christ's death and burial and resurrection, take some time to read through the book of Matthew.

Reflect: How do you think Jesus' sacrifice on the cross changes your ability to have peace?

Record Your Thoughts

Prayer: Thank You, Lord, for loving me so much that you sent the gift of Jesus, who died on the cross for my sin in my place. I believe that because of the gift of His life, I can now have a relationship with you. Amen.

Power Prayer for Week 2: Thank You, Father, for making a way for me to have peace.

Day 5

My babies were finally sleeping, and I was downstairs in the sewing room trying to focus on my next slipcover job. It was a wing chair. As I pinned the fabric in place, a pit rose in my stomach —it was a knot welling up from the bottom and rising in my throat. It tightened, almost taking my breath away, leaving me with a half-paralyzed feeling. I sat down on the floor, cried out, "God, where is this coming from? I can't live in this pit of darkness over me."

I didn't know where my feelings of panic and paralysis were coming from or why I was experiencing them. I couldn't label the feeling as fear. It just felt like a looming, black shadow. It felt the exact opposite of what I believed peace to be.

Though I had been a Christian most of my life, the shadowy feeling was familiar. It was something I had felt pretty much every day for as long as I could remember. By this time in my life, I knew it wasn't of God. Dark clouds and paralysis built up over the years, creating a stronghold.

God began to reveal to me a root. Shortly after my middle child was born, I quit my part-time job to stay home with the kids and work on my sewing business. I was nervous about the finances, as I would no longer have a set paycheck coming in each week. While I was sewing I would have a mental check list of my tasks along with the projected income from each project. Most weeks, it didn't seem like it would be enough, which would trigger memories of the financial instability and food insecurity of my childhood. Immediately my thoughts and emotions became overcome with fear. Even though our financial situation was far more stable than my younger years I couldn't control the panic that set in when the fear overtook me.

Circumstances and feelings from my childhood had gone unchecked for so long that they were serious strongholds that the devil held over me. In Bible terms, I could refer to it as a stronghold. In scientific terms, these were toxic memory trees growing in my brain. I didn't yet understand the psychology of how our amygdala triggers a fight and flight response within our brains. For years, I had criticized myself for allowing these "strongholds" to control.

I believe in Christian circles we do a disservice by referring to our inner turmoil only in spiritual terms without recognizing and working through the science of how God formed our mind, will, soul, and emotions. When you understand the way God created these parts to work together, you will gain wisdom and understanding about the root issues with which you are struggling and how to process them.

God began teaching me to focus on Him one day at a time. When the panic came, He would lead me to Scripture to repeat over and over to battle my thoughts. For these fears it was, "Thank You for giving me my daily bread."

Read: 2 Timothy 1:7, "For the Spirit God gave us does not make us timid, but gives us power, love and self-discipline."

Reflect: Can you relate to feelings of overwhelm, panic, paralyzing fear, or darkness? Journal some about this and think about when it occurs.

Record Your Thoughts

Prayer: Father, I believe that You have not given me the spirit of fear, but of love, power, and a sound mind. I recognize I experienced (name some things from your past). I ask for your help in overcoming these memories. In Jesus' name, Amen.

Power Prayer for Week 2: Thank You, Father, for making a way for me to have peace.

Day 6

When I took the sewing machine from the box on the first day of sewing club, I couldn't help but laugh when one girl said to the other, "I'm really skilled at sewing by hand; I've been practicing for two weeks already!"

Children believe they can perfect a skill in two weeks. Yet, as adults, we all know that isn't true. Perhaps you've heard the general statement that it takes 10,000 hours of practice to become an expert, which is a concept explained in Malcom Gladwell's book "The Outliers." Whether 10,000 hours is exactly right doesn't really matter if we recognize that becoming an expert takes a lot of work and practice, both of which are a sacrifice of time and comfort.

It takes time and repetition to cultivate a peaceful heart and mind. Peace doesn't come without sacrifice. In the Old Testament, a peace offering was required. In the New Testament, Jesus gave His life. Though peace is fully available to us through Jesus, we must sacrifice time and energy to pursue it. It isn't just a matter of "doing" more Christian things.

Romans 12:1-2 exhorts us to present our bodies as a living sacrifice, so that we might know the will of God. Second Corinthians 10:5 teaches us to destroy things in our mind that lead us away from knowing God. The fears I mentioned in yesterday's reading were leading me away from believing God. Rather than holding on to Scripture I was allowing past experience to determine my view of the future. It was a sacrifice to surrender my fearful thoughts in exchange for His Word.

My sacrifice looked like a continual conversation with God, "God, I'm afraid. I will not fear tomorrow because You promise to provide my daily bread. I know that You are with me and trust You to take care of today."

Peace comes when we know God and His will from our heart, not just our head. His will is that we trust Him. This trust is part of the sacrifice we make to fight for our peace of mind. We can engage in this fight for our peace when, with God's help (and often the help of others), we recognize what is in our minds that is keeping us from knowing Christ. As we go through this devotional, there will be much more about this topic. For now, let's remember that it will take some work—it may take 10,000 hours of concentrated effort.

Read: Romans 12:1-2, "Therefore, I urge you, brothers and sisters, in view of God's mercy, to offer your bodies as a living sacrifice, holy and pleasing to God—this is your true and proper worship. Do not conform to the pattern of this world, but be transformed by the renewing of your mind. Then you will be able to test and approve what God's will is—his good, pleasing and perfect will."

2 Corinthians 10:4-5, "The weapons we fight with are not the weapons of the world. On the contrary, they have divine power to demolish strongholds. We demolish arguments and every pretension that sets itself up against the knowledge of God, and we take captive every thought to make it obedient to Christ."

Reflect: What is one thing that has taken you a lot of work or effort to learn and master?

Record Your Thoughts

Prayer: Father, I am often in a hurry to check things off my list. Help me continually pursue Your peace and put forth effort to fight the battle of my thoughts. Thank You that You are in it with me, giving me the strength and perseverance I need. Amen.

Power Prayer for Week 2: Thank You, Father, for making a way for me to have peace.

Week 3: The Power of Belief

Thank You for being my Good Shepherd, providing me rest, nourishment, and all that I need.

Day 1

After church, a petite lady approached me. "So, you sew?" she asked with awe in her voice.

"Yes," I replied. "I learned to sew as a kid."

She told me that because she is short, she always needs to have pants shortened. I commented I would be happy to teach her how to hem her own pants. In reply, she said she couldn't. Her great aunt sewed beautifully and had tried to teach her, but it just didn't work out. She just didn't have the knack for it and couldn't learn.

Every woman seems to have a sewing story. In that story, she made an unconscious decision about her ability to sew. Tapping into these stories is the first step of learning, because there is power in what we believe to be true (regardless of whether it is true). We act on what we believe to be true. An attitude of defeat and incompetence will most certainly lead to defeat.

One day, as a young mom with an infant and a toddler, I felt overwhelmed with the responsibilities of life and parenting. My overwhelm grew into frustration and anger as these words raged within me, "I can't do this! I don't have the strength to be a parent. I'm not cut out to be a stay-at-home mom."

At church on Sunday mornings, I affirmed I believed in the power of Jesus. I would sing songs like, "There's Power in the Blood," but God began showing me that belief comes from the heart and affects how I live. Did I believe He had power over my day-to-day life? I wasn't attempting a grandiose life of self-sacrifice. There were no moves in the future. I could work from home, and honestly, I should have felt blessed by the life that I was leading.

Yet all I felt was stress.

Through this God began challenging me to give thanks. As I nursed my infant daughter in the middle of the night, I devoured the words of Ann Voskamp, in her book "One Thousand Gifts." Long after the baby had fallen asleep in my arms I kept reading. I wanted to learn this thanksgiving.

Read: Philippians 4:6-9, "Do not be anxious about anything, but in every situation, by prayer and petition, with thanksgiving, present your requests to God. And the peace of God, which transcends all understanding, will guard your hearts and your minds in Christ Jesus.

Finally, brothers and sisters, whatever is true, whatever is noble, whatever is right, whatever is pure, whatever is lovely, whatever is admirable—if anything is excellent or praiseworthy—think about such things. Whatever you have learned or received or heard from me, or seen in me—put it into practice. And the God of peace will be with you."

Reflect: List out some of your worries. Ask God to show you what you need and how to give thanks in your current situation.

Record Your Thoughts

Prayer: Lord, Thank You for a brand-new day. You know that (name your problem) is something that is worrying me. I believe You are already working in this situation. Help me keep my eyes fixed on You. Amen.

Power Prayer for Week 3: Thank You for being my Good Shepherd, providing me rest, nourishment, and all that I need.

Day 2

As a pre-teen, my family spent about six months living with my grandparents in Maine. As soon as we settled, my grandmother (Granna was her chosen grandmotherly name) made sure that the sewing machine found a home in my bedroom. It was one of those machines that was built into the table. I promptly began aspiring to all the projects I could make with it. Of course, it's only natural that I should start with big dreams, so I chose a twin quilt. Granna graciously donated a closet full of Grampa's old shirts for the project, and I set to work. I had no pattern—just this concept of 12 x 12 squares made up of various geometric shapes.

I had the childlike faith that I was able. I could make a quilt if I set my mind to it. I was not yet bound by the harsh judgment of my perfection that often enters with adulthood.

Isn't this the picture that Jesus painted of children? In the book of Matthew, He brings the children up on His lap, and proclaims that unless we become humble like little children, we will not enter the kingdom of heaven (Matthew 18).

In childhood we hold a simpler, more trusting view of life making it easier to have faith, or to be content with imperfections. As we get older, disappointments, grief, and challenges test our faith through lived experiences. We become more cognizant of how hard the world is. Often, the impossibility of something or the sheer size of a task may make us want to shrink back in fear of moving forward.

It is not belief in us, but the humility to believe in God who is able. One day, a man brought his demon-possessed son to Jesus, asking for deliverance for the boy. Yet his petition ended with the words, "if you can." Jesus questioned this: did the father really believe? Then the father recognized his own unbelief and asked God for help to believe (Mark 9:24).

To live in peace, belief is foundational. We must work at training our heart to believe like a little child, asking for God to help us in our unbelief.

Read: Matthew 18:1-6, "At that time the disciples came to Jesus and asked, "Who, then, is the greatest in the kingdom of heaven?" He called a little child to him, and placed the child among them. And he said: "Truly I tell you, unless you change and become like little children, you will never enter the kingdom ofheaven. Therefore, whoever takes the lowly position of this child is the greatest in the kingdom of heaven. And whoever welcomes one such child in my name welcomes me. "If anyone causes one of these little ones—those who believe in me—to stumble, it would be better for them to have a large millstone hung around their neck and to be drowned in the depths of the sea.

Optional Additional Reading: Mark 9:14-29

Reflect: Are there ways in which you think you have a childlike faith? What areas do you feel you struggle to find hope and belief?

Record Your Thoughts

Prayer: Father God, I want to believe with the audacity of a little child, but I struggle to believe for so many reasons. In my heart I struggle to believe that You are a good Father—that You are for me and that You have a good, meaningful plan for my life. I ask for help in my unbelief. Amen.

Power Prayer for Week 3: Thank You for being my Good Shepherd, providing me rest, nourishment, and all that I need.

Day 3

As a young homemaker, I set out to make a set of calico curtains for our apartment. I also wanted to add a lining to them so the room would darken for sleeping when they were closed. When I purchased the fabrics, I knew they were both 100% cotton. I also knew that most sewists recommend pre-washing the fabric to prevent shrinkage during future washing. But I was in too much of a hurry. The fabric was so crisp right from the store—so easy to cut, without having to iron it after the pre-washing stage. So, I disregarded the advice of the experts and made the curtains without preshrinking.

The curtains became skewed after the first washing. The lining did not shrink in equal percentage to the calico curtain fabric. I had the skills to sew but refused to act on what I knew.

Did you know that if you know the right thing to do and refuse to do it, the Bible calls it sin? (James 4:17) Also, if you say you believe something to be true but then do the opposite, you create a cognitive dissonance within your belief. If you believe something, you must act out of that belief, because mental assent to that belief is not enough.

One of my biggest challenges with acting on the faith I profess was my fear and insecurity. For example, as believers, sometimes we may feel "led" to do something and believe God directed us. However, often the feeling may be rooted in our fears and insecurities.

When I felt God leading me to leave my day job to only work at my business, I had many fears. I did not have my business built up as much as I wanted and didn't know how we would make ends meet. Yet, I had the example of the Israelites as God led them out of Egypt to the Promised Land. From day to day, they didn't know how they would be fed, but God provided them with the daily bread of manna. If I believed He was leading me to take this step, as the same God who provided for the Israelites who would also provide for me, I had to choose how I would act. The choice was mine: act on my own fears or act on what I believed to be true about God.

As I refused to do things the right way, I ruined the curtains. How often do we blame God when things don't work out? Yet may we ask ourselves the question—did we act in faith or listen to our fears when we heard His voice?

Read: 2 Timothy 1:7, "For the Spirit God gave us does not make us timid, but gives us power, love and self-discipline."

Optional Additional Reading: James 2:14-26

Reflection: In what ways do you sense the Holy Spirit showing you that you are acting out of fear rather than faith?

Record Your Thoughts

Prayer: Father, I ask for forgiveness for the times that I have acted out of fear rather than faith. I want to walk in faith, but I struggle to believe when I'm in the middle of a challenging situation. I pray You will help my unbelief, Thank You for filling me with faith. Amen.

Power Prayer for Week 3: Thank You for being my Good Shepherd, providing me rest, nourishment, and all that I need.

Day 4

I cannot count how many times I have heard the words, "I can't sew," over the years. People often follow the words with a lengthy story about why they can't sew. The highlight of the story is always their failure and their conclusion that they can't do it. We often frame our proclamations of "can't" based on our experience, rather than on an unwavering belief that God can.

Like sewing stories, we all have life stories—the events, upbringing and circumstances of life that have affected the moments of our days. From these, we form a personal narrative. I was so close to falling into mother-hood, business, writing and life with the narrative of "can't." My experience told me I couldn't because I felt overwhelmed, frustrated and exhausted.

What if we could change the narratives of the story by the words we speak? If we confess with our mouth and believe in our heart that God raised Him from the dead, Romans 10:9 says that we will be saved. The Greek word used here for confess is homologeo, which according to Strong's concordance literally means "to speak the same thing."

I had previously thought of this verse as only pertaining to the initial act of coming to know Christ as my Savior. You know, the Sunday School version of praying to God and confessing Him as Lord, so I would be assured of going to heaven when I died. You can call me greedy, but I want-ed more than salvation from hell. I desperately wanted to be saved from my overwhelm and mom guilt.

Belief is about speaking what He says into our daily life, rather than what we see and feel in the natural world. Repeatedly through the Bible, God talked about bestowing strength on His people. Though the problem at hand was my inability to mother, my theology had to change as well. Did I believe Jesus died so that I could experience a relationship with God now? I'm talking about the good relationship—the kind where you want to call your dad and just sit on his lap for a hug like you did as a child. Did I believe He was a present, active part of my daily life?

The words of Psalm 23 pour over me in the King James version just as I learned them as a child. "The Lord is my shepherd; I shall not want. He leads me besides still waters, He makes me lie down in green pastures, He restores my soul."

I grabbed onto them as a confession with a heart open. I cried out, wrestling to believe. I prayed, "Lord, I believe You are my shepherd. I believe what You say, that You will lead me beside still waters, that You will restore my soul."

Read: Romans 10:9-10, " If you declare with your mouth, "Jesus is Lord," and believe in your heart that God raised him from the dead, you will be saved. For it is with your heart that you believe and are justified, and it is with your mouth that you profess your faith and are saved."

Reflect: Think about the words you speak. Are you speaking (confessing) what God says about your situation, or do you notice yourself speaking fear, anxiety, and distrust?

Record Your Thoughts

Prayer: Lord, forgive me for the words that I have spoken in negativity. I ask that You help me guard the words that I speak and only speak words that have faith and belief in You. Amen.

Power Prayer for Week 3: Thank You for being my Good Shepherd, providing me rest, nourishment, and all that I need.

Day 5

I stared at the pictures on my Facebook messenger of a wedding gown six sizes too big. It was a gown with a mesh bodice and lace overlay. Could I do the job? I wasn't sure. I wanted to doubt. But I reflected on my two decades of sewing. I had made dresses from scratch and altered hundreds (if not thousands) more. With a deep breath, I reminded myself that I had the skills and typed back a response, "Yes, I'll do it."

In Joshua 4, Joshua built an altar to the Lord as a remembrance of what God had done. He had brought the people of Israel across the Jordan River. This altar or monument was a place of remembrance so that they could recall what God had done. When we stop to count the faithfulness that we have seen in our lifetime, it builds our faith.

When I looked at a dress that was six sizes too big and extremely complicated, I felt scared. I doubted my ability. Everything within me wanted to respond out of my own doubts. But when I reminded myself of the truth that I had the skills, I had confidence or faith. In the same way, the everyday circumstances or challenges of our lives can cause us to doubt when we look at them for too long. Instead, purposefully count the things that God has done, remind Him of the promises that He has made and the faithfulness that you have seen Him do. If you can't think of anything that you have seen Him do in your life, look at the lives of those in the Bible. Remind God that He provided manna (bread) for the Israelites and that you believe He will also provide for you.

Focusing on the faithfulness of God is a choice that will ultimately have power over our doubts. We must settle the belief in our own minds—do we doubt, or do we believe God?

The famous preacher Charles Spurgeon wrote, "Truth must enter into the soul, penetrating and saturating it or else it is of no value. Doctrine accepted simply as a matter of a system or belief is like bread in one's hand, providing no nourishment to the body whatsoever. But doctrine accepted by the heart is like food digested. Truth must be a living force."[6]

When we grab hold of God's truth with belief, rather than doubt, it becomes a living force within us.

Read: James 1:5-8, "If any of you lacks wisdom, you should ask God, who gives generously to all without finding fault, and it will be given to you. But when you ask, you must believe and not doubt, because the one who doubts is like a wave of the sea, blown and tossed by the wind. That person should not expect to receive anything from the Lord. Such a person is double-minded and unstable in all they do."
Optional Additional Reading: Joshua 4

Reflection: In what ways have you seen God work in your past before? What are the specific things that you are struggling to trust Him to work in today?

Record Your Thoughts

Prayer: For this prayer, make it directly related to how you have seen God work or how He worked before. Make it personal to you. This is an example:

At one point I prayed persistently for a husband, and I saw God provide. In the thing that I am praying for or believing God to work in now, I can remind God of His faithfulness then by praying, "Lord, thank You for Your faithfulness in providing my husband when I was praying for him. You have shown Your great love and faithfulness to me in the past. I believe You will prove yourself faithful again."

If you can't think of any area of your life that you have seen God work, you can pull an account from the Scripture, such as from Joshua 4. "Lord, You caused the Jordan River to stop flowing, so the Ark of the Covenant could go across. I believe You are the same today as You were then, and I believe You desire to act on my behalf. I long to see Your faithfulness to me in (my situation). I praise You for being the faithful One who never fails. Amen."

Power Prayer for Week 3: Thank You for being my Good Shepherd, providing me rest, nourishment, and all that I need.

Day 6

After my husband volunteered my services to sew slipcovers for an acquaintance, I began working with bulk zipper—as in yards and yards of zipper—that I cut to size for slipcover cushions. This zipper didn't come with the pulls attached. I had to measure out the zipper length, then separate the two strands of teeth. Each side of the zipper would get sewn separately to its respective piece of fabric. After that stitching was done, I had to line up the base of the teeth with the zipper pull and evenly pull the two sides of the zipper through the pull. Without the pull attached and aligned, the zipper could not do its job of bringing the two sides together.

It was challenging. I'm not sure why I struggled with it so much, but this caused me some trouble over the years. However, it was a necessity. Without the zipper pull properly attached, the pull couldn't perform its intended purpose.

If you have spent any time reading the Bible and in Christian circles, it is likely that you have a bit of knowledge. This knowledge is like zipper strands. Maybe you have done a great job stitching it to the fabric by memorizing the Bible and developing good moral habits. But what pulls it together to make our lives whole is belief.

I wonder if we live our lives as two halves of a zipper that are still disconnected. On one side we have the words of the Bible, Jesus, and the example of all those men and women of faith within its pages. On the other half of the zipper is our current life with its stressors and challenges and unique situations. If we learned to pull the two sides together, would we not be forming that mind/heart connection that would make our lives a representation of the faith we say we have?

We may think we believe, yet a closer look at our words, actions, and mindset may reveal that what we say we believe is not lining up with how we are living. This creates a cognitive dissonance within ourselves, which will cause internal anxiety. The soul cannot enter a state of rest with this type of disconnect, which will keep you from experiencing true peace.

As you move forward in peace it is important to intentionally nurture belief. This is done by strengthening the mind/heart connection by choosing your words and actions to reflect the truth of Scripture. This will teach your mind, will, and emotions to focus on God's truth in your everyday life.

Read: Psalm 19:14, "May these words of my mouth and this meditation of my heart be pleasing in your sight, Lord, my Rock and my Redeemer."

Matthew 22:37, "Jesus replied: 'Love the Lord your God with all your heart and with all your soul and with all your mind.'"

Reflect: What are some key things you have learned about how your words and your thoughts affect your belief? How will you put this into practice?

Record Your Thoughts

Prayer: Thank You, Lord, for showing me the disconnect between my words and thoughts and my faith. Help me pause before I speak and let my words reflect my trust in You. Help me recognize the thoughts that bring doubt and teach my mind to believe. Amen.

Power Prayer for Week 3: Thank You for being my Good Shepherd, providing me rest, nourishment, and all that I need.

Week 4: Jesus as The Teacher of Peace

Thank You, Father, for giving me Jesus, the Prince of Peace, as my teacher of peace.

Day 1

I dreamed of making my wedding gown. Shortly after my engagement I fell in love with a pattern: bell sleeves and an empire waist. Satin and chiffon were not fabrics I was comfortable working with, so I paid for private lessons to improve my skills. During these lessons, I made a satin pant suit, making sure I was comfortable with that type of fabric. I learned special pressing techniques, the finesse of easing, and several other couture methods that gave me the confidence I needed. Learning from a teacher made all the difference.

In the Christian life, we also benefit from a teacher. Often, we look to pastors, Sunday School teachers and Christian authors for the knowledge we long to gain. Philosopher Dallas Willard writes we should embrace Christ as our Teacher.[7] He points out the ideology that the life of faith in Christ should be one of abundance and obedience, but we have no bridge from the faith to life. We fall into faith as a religion that we must learn about rather than a relationship from which we learn.

Do we see Jesus as merely our Savior as we try to do the work ourselves? Even in my faith background, perhaps I relied heavily on the teachings of Christ without letting Him come close enough to be my teacher.

To have a teacher naturally means that we must become students (i.e. disciples) of the teacher. To become a student of Christ, who is better to be our teacher of peace than the Prince of Peace Himself? From teachers, we learn by their example their words, actions, interactions, and instruction.

I do not always come to Him with a teachable spirit. The words of the psalmist become an example as I pray, "Show me your ways, Lord, teach me Your paths. Guide me in Your truth and teach me" (Psalm 25:4-5a). We are prone to want our own way. Asking Him to teach us is a form of worship and surrender, acknowledging our need for Him. In pursuit of peace, this week we will learn from Jesus' example.

Read: Matthew 4:23, "Jesus went throughout Galilee, teaching in their synagogues, proclaiming the good news of the kingdom, and healing every disease and sickness among the people."

Matthew 5:2, "and he [Jesus] began to teach them."

Matthew 7:29, "Because he taught as one who had authority, and not as their teachers of the law."

Reflect: In these passages what does Jesus do? Have you ever thought of Jesus as your teacher? What would you like to learn from Him? How can you have a teachable spirit?

Record Your Thoughts

Prayer: Thank you, Father, that Jesus is my teacher. Help me to learn from His life, His teaching and His example. Amen.

Power Prayer for Week 4: Thank You, Father, for giving me Jesus, the Prince of Peace, as my teacher of peace.

Day 2

Several months ago, I ripped the belt loop on a favorite pair of pants. The belt loop wasn't the only part that was damaged. When the belt loop came off, it ripped the fabric of the pants. A glaring hole revealed my underwear. After the pants ripped, I folded them and put them on the chest at the end of my bed. A month later, they moved into the sewing room on the table. Another few weeks later, I piled them with some of my other personal mending and set them on a shelf. There they sit. It's been a good four months since they ripped.

In podcasts and on my YouTube channel, I talk a lot about the benefits of mending as good stewards of our financial resources and the role it plays in reducing environmental waste. I say that I want to fix them. If I truly want to fix them, why haven't I?

Ask the question. Do you want peace? Why don't you have it?

Jesus, our Teacher, asked a similar question. He had the gall to ask a man who was an invalid for 38 years if he wanted to get well (John 5:6).

The question seems ridiculous, but sometimes teachers ask questions to get us to think. They want us to see the root of an issue or to reveal our heart attitude. Sometimes questions like this will lead us to the root of an issue.

To wear my pants again, I must do more than want them to be fixed. I must sit and sew them. We may say that we want peace, but along with wanting it, perhaps we need to take the question a bit more seriously. Does the desire for peace stir us into action?

When I examine my heart, I recognize the times that I become comfortable with the way things are, even if it isn't what's best. Perhaps the invalid in the Bible story became comfortable in his identity as an invalid. Maybe he had made friends with those who surrounded him in a familiar setting. Even though we may want peace as opposed to anxiety, the drama within our own souls may be the norm, and it feels comfortable. It takes no effort to stay in that familiar place, but leaving it is unknown territory.

With Jesus as our teacher and example, let us ask the hard questions—the seemingly ridiculous questions—until we reach the root and become stirred to act.

Read: John 5:1-9, "Some time later, Jesus went up to Jerusalem for one of the Jewish festivals. Now there is in Jerusalem near the Sheep Gate a pool, which in Aramaic is called Bethesda and which is surrounded by five covered colonnades. Here a great number of disabled people used to lie—the blind, the lame, the paralyzed. One who was there had been an invalid for thirty-eight years. When Jesus saw him lying there and learned that he had been in this condition for a long time, he asked him, 'Do you want to get well?'

'Sir,' the invalid replied, 'I have no one to help me into the pool when the water is stirred. While I am trying to get in, someone else goes down ahead of me.'

Then Jesus said to him, 'Get up! Pick up your mat and walk.' At once the man was cured; he picked up his mat and walked."

Reflect: Do you want a more peaceful heart? Why? What might God call you to leave or do in to pursue peace? Do you have friends who speak anxiety or fear over you? Is the drama of an anxious heart familiar to you?

Record Your Thoughts

Prayer: Thank you, Lord, for challenging me with the hard questions. I want to be teachable. Help me take an honest look at my heart and act on what I know to be true. Amen.

Power Prayer for Week 4: Thank You, Father, for giving me Jesus, the Prince of Peace, as my teacher of peace.

Day 3

I was so excited to use my new serger. New to the sewing business, I purchased the serger for a more professional touch. This way, I could finish the edges after trimming the seams of an alteration. I had just finished narrowing the leg width of a firefighter's pants and brought them over to the machine. With enthusiasm, I pressed down on the pedal and sped down the pant leg. The serger was so fast! As I removed the pants from the machine, I felt pleased with the stitch. However, upon flipping the leg, I noticed the extra fabric folded into the seam. While fixing the mistake, I found the serger's sharp cutter had sliced a hole in the tangled leg seam. This pair of pants was not fixable. Have you ever noticed hurry rarely ends well?

Jesus was never in a hurry. Have you ever thought about that? Several years ago, an author pointed this out in a book I was reading (my sincere apologies for not recalling which one to credit the author.) This truth stuck with me—Jesus was never in a hurry.

When Jesus was 12, he went to the Passover festival with His parents. As they headed home, He stayed behind with the religious teachers, talking in the Temple. His parents spent three days looking for Him. When they questioned why He had let them worry so much, He responded by asking why they were surprised that He was engaged in His Father's work. From Luke 2:41-52, one notable observation is Jesus' lack of urgency to return home. He wasn't in a hurry to carry out the travel plans. He wasn't in a hurry to leave the spiritual conversations He was having at the temple.

I was always in a hurry. Not just in activity, but also an impatience with time and waiting. I am not alone in this. I hear the constant complaints of those around me, "I'm so busy" or "I don't have time." Is this how we want to live? In my life, I see how deadlines, activities, and events can drive me to rush through life. I want to live unhurried like Jesus did. One way that I have learned to live unhurried is to purposefully build margin into my schedule, which you will learn about in later weeks.

Read: John 11:1-7, "Now a man named Lazarus was sick. He was from Bethany, the village of Mary and her sister Martha. (This Mary, whose brother Lazarus now lay sick, was the same one who poured perfume on the Lord and wiped his feet with her hair.) So the sisters sent word to Jesus, 'Lord, the one you love is sick.'

When he heard this, Jesus said, 'This sickness will not end in death. No, it is for God's glory so that God's Son may be glorified through it.' Now Jesus loved Martha and her sister and Lazarus. So when he heard that Lazarus was sick, he stayed where he was two more days, and then he said to his disciples, 'Let us go back to Judea.'"

Reflect: When were you hurried in the past few days? How is the state of peace within yourself when you feel hurried? Why do you hurry so much? Did Jesus hurry to see Lazarus?

Record Your Thoughts

Prayer: Lord, thank You for Jesus, who was never in a hurry. I want to learn from Him. As I read the Scripture and continue to grow spiritually, help me to recognize the areas of life in which I am hurried. I ask for Your wisdom and understanding of ways in which I can cultivate a less hurried life.

Power Prayer for Week 4: Thank You, Father, for giving me Jesus, the Prince of Peace, as my teacher of peace.

Day 4

When the kids were little, bedtime was promptly at 7:00 p.m. Once they were asleep, I headed downstairs to the sewing room to work for several hours. My husband was also in bed early as he had to leave for work at 1:30 a.m. The house was quiet. Only the sewing machine broke the silence. These hours of quiet sewing became some of my most precious times of the day. There in the silence I could connect to my Father through prayer, worship songs, audio books, podcasts and sometimes simply silence. During these times of silence my spiritual life gained strength and courage. In the silence, I felt God's presence and clear direction from Him.

Jesus was also a great example in His pursuit of silence with His Father. Many times in Scripture, we see Jesus separating Himself from the crowd and turning to silence. In Mark 1:35, He rose early to pray. In Luke 5:16, Jesus withdrew from the crowds to pray. There are more instances, but in Jesus' example, I see how His time alone with the Father gave Him strength for His ministry.

As Jesus ministered to the crowds, I can imagine how overwhelming it might have been for all those people to need Him. Between marriage, business, motherhood, friendship, and writing, I always felt needed, and the overwhelm was real. I'm sure you also experience the demands of people around you in your life. The word "overwhelmed" is a common feeling in our society.

Overwhelm feels and sounds exactly opposite to the feeling of peace. Overwhelm feels like my inner self running, rushing, and drowning through the thousands of voices and demands. In overwhelm I lose my center, forget the purpose of my life and think that I am responsible for it all.

If you feel overwhelmed, peace may seem impossible. What do you do? Do you keep running on the hamster wheel of life? What would it look like to withdraw to stillness with your Father? As we look back to the Father chapter, let's remember that we must firmly root our faith (and peace) in our attachment to God as our Father.

When I am overwhelmed, I find myself running to Him. I have found that He is a good Father who is able to orchestrate the moments of my days by taking things off my agenda or filling me with strength for a task when I am weary. Run to Him when you feel overwhelmed and lay your burden down.

Read: Luke 5:12-16, "While Jesus was in one of the towns, a man came along who was covered with leprosy. When he saw Jesus, he fell with his face to the ground and begged him, 'Lord, if you are willing, you can make me clean.'

Jesus reached out his hand and touched the man. 'I am willing,' he said. 'Be clean!' And immediately the leprosy left him.

Then Jesus ordered him, 'Don't tell anyone, but go, show yourself to the priest and offer the sacrifices that Moses commanded for your cleansing, as a testimony to them.'

Yet the news about him spread all the more, so that crowds of people came to hear him and to be healed of their sicknesses. But Jesus often withdrew to lonely places and prayed."

Reflect: Note Jesus' actions. In what ways do you feel overwhelmed or crowded by noise?

Record Your Thoughts

Prayer: Father, I feel overwhelmed. I long to quiet my heart in Your silence. Give me a hunger for Your peace, as I work to seek You in times of overwhelm. Amen.

Power Prayer for Week 4: Thank You, Father, for giving me Jesus, the Prince of Peace, as my teacher of peace.

Day 5

During my final year of pursing my bachelor's degree, I took a non-profit marketing class and could research the marketing plan of any organization I chose. The idea of serving God through sewing has fascinated me. A Google search of sewing ministries led me to Enchanted Makeovers in Taylor, Michigan. Through this, I connected with founder and CEO Terry Grahl. Besides creating beauty in shelters to give a sense of hope, the organization also engages volunteers in sewing capes for kids. Handmade gifts of love act as a superpower. They give a child the belief that someone values them. What stuck with me most from my conversations with Ms. Grahl was her phrase, "Serve with your talents."

Did you know that serving others can decrease the stress that we feel, which automatically gives us a greater sense of peace? Taryn Fernandes, MD, a supervising physician at MEDvidi (an online mental health treatment center), explains, "Studies have shown that helping others can decrease cortisol, the stress hormone, while increasing oxytocin, related to positive social interactions and generosity."[8]

Jesus our Teacher was the epitome of a servant to others. He welcomed the children, fed the hungry, provided wine for a wedding, and healed the sick. Jesus employed the gifts He received, along with the power, love, and compassion given to Him by His Father, to serve others. He knew His purpose was to serve.

Besides sewing, I also like to cook and write cards. I would consider those as gifts or talents that I have. When I find myself overwhelmed, stressed, and feeling sorry for myself, I have learned to step back and ask God who I can bless today. God always puts someone on my heart. Sometimes, it's a neighbor or friend who would appreciate a home-cooked meal or an encouraging card. These acts quickly transform my inner stress to calm, joy, and peace.

Serving takes the focus of our energy off ourselves and turns to blessing others. Ephesians 6:7-8 is a reminder that what we do for others is an act of serving the Lord. Serving is a form of worship, which builds your connection to Father God.

Read: John 13:13-16, (Just after Jesus has washed the disciples' feet) "You call me 'Teacher' and 'Lord,' and rightly so, for that is what I am. Now that I, your Lord and Teacher, have washed your feet, you also should wash one another's feet. I have set you an example that you should do as I have done for you. Very truly I tell you, no servant is greater than his master, nor is a messenger greater than the one who sent him."

Reflect: Write what stands out to you about serving from this passage. What are some of your talents? Brainstorm some simple ways that you could use your talents to serve others.

Record Your Thoughts

Prayer: Lord, thank You for the gifts and talents that You have given me. Help me find creative ways to be a blessing to those I know. Amen.

Power Prayer for Week 4: Thank You, Father, for giving me Jesus, the Prince of Peace, as my teacher of peace.

Day 6

As I worked with a teacher during my one-on-one sewing lessons, my skills improved. After several months, I had the confidence to tackle my wedding gown. Without applying my teacher's lessons, the classes would have been useless. In the same way, if we do not apply the lessons of Christ to our daily lives, the learning is useless.

The great news about Jesus as our Teacher is that He isn't asking for a financial investment for each class (though the biblical practice of tithing and giving cheerfully is something He taught consistently). He wants us to become disciples. According to Strong's Concordance, the word disciple refers to someone who "was not only a pupil, but an adherent; hence they are spoken of as imitators of their teacher."[9] Becoming a disciple means imitating his example. Listening to teaching does not make us disciples—putting the teaching into practice does.

This week we have focused on four prime examples from the life of Christ as our Teacher: living unhurried, asking questions to find the root, pursuing silence, and practicing service. To truly experience God's peace, these four steps are just the beginning. These may seem unfamiliar to you. Remember the man who couldn't walk for 38 years. Perhaps the disability had become comfortable for him. Perhaps he forgot what it was like to be well. Maybe he wondered if the "normal" members of society would accept him.

Following our Teacher may feel like an unfamiliar path. Living unhurried, pursuing silence, and taking the time to examine our hearts with deep questions are abnormal in our society. I am constantly faced with choices about how to use my time and in what activities to be involved. Rather than jumping to sign up for another activity, I try to pause and ask for God's wisdom about the commitment.

Our schedules reflect our priorities. Taking time to be with Him gives Him the opportunity to do the work in You. This also trains our minds to know that He is the most important priority on our schedule and He can orchestrate our to-do list and give us the strength that we need. It also fosters quiet space in which we can ask deep questions.

Read: John 8:31-32, "To the Jews who had believed him, Jesus said, 'If you hold to my teaching, you are really my disciples. Then you will know the truth, and the truth will set you free.'"

Reflect: Do you want peace? Are you willing to implement the wisdom of the Teacher and take the less familiar path? Review your notes from these four topics through this past week.

Eliminating hurry

Pursuing silence

Asking deep questions

Serving

How willing are you to practice these?

Record Your Thoughts

Prayer: Father, I want peace in my life. These practices don't seem familiar to me. I don't know how to change or how to believe that I can change. I believe You have the power to change me, and that You are calling me to be Your disciple and truly follow Your teachings. Amen.

Power Prayer for Week 4: Thank You, Father, for giving me Jesus, the Prince of Peace, as my teacher of peace.

Week 5: Trust Brings Peace

Thank You for Your truth which conquers my fears.

Day 1

Claire Hunte writes, "Sewing is a visual language. It has a voice. It has been used by people to communicate something of themselves—their history, beliefs, prayers, and protests."[10] All this is conveyed using needle and thread with intricate patterns and fabrics.

The state of our heart and the beliefs that we hold are also visual languages. Those looking in can trace the threads of our lives to determine if we have woven them in peace or in confusion and anxiety. One foundation to stitching a life reflecting the peace of God is belief and trust.

During the first week, I laid the foundation of attachment—our need to attach to God as our Father. The purpose of Christianity is that we may know Him and be close to Him. The purpose of sewing is to join pieces together securely, create beauty with embroidery, and patch holes.

In faith, we must choose belief that will draw us into knowing God. Jesus said in John 14:1, "Don't let your hearts be troubled. Trust in God, and trust also in me." (NLT) The word for trust here is "pisteuo" which also means to entrust. Strong's Concordance states that entrusting one's spiritual wellbeing to Christ involves not only believing but also being persuaded and placing confidence in Him. It signifies reliance upon Him, rather than mere credence, and is therefore translated as "commit unto," "commit one's trust," or "be committed unto."[11]

As a Sunday School kid, I was taught "belief" in Jesus, Old Testament heroes, and New Testament apostles. But the belief was a credence. In childhood, we rarely know the difference between being taught something as words versus theology. But to adhere to Christ as more than a credence—to really wrestle with Scripture tenaciously until we believe from our heart, not just our head—that takes maturity beyond our child years.

As we enter adulthood, questions may come, and our inner persons will recognize the cognitive dissonance between what we say we believe (adhere to) versus what we actually do. This past Sunday at church our pastor reminded us this difference, asking the congregation members to hold up their Bibles and repeat several statements of belief including, "This is my Bible, I believe by faith what is written, I'm what it says I am, I can be what it says I can be, I can do what it says I can do, to the Glory of His name and Kingdom!"

How often our faith becomes more like rote knowledge than belief and trust that comes from deep within. We want faith to be reflected in all that we are.

Read: John 14:1-4, "Do not let your hearts be troubled. You believe in God; believe also in me. My Father's house has many rooms; if that were not so, would I have told you that I am going there to prepare a place for you? And if I go and prepare a place for you, I will come back and take you to be with me that you also may be where I am. You know the way to the place where I am going."

Reflect: Are you anxious or afraid?

Consider reading further in John 14. Notice how many times this passage mentions trust and belief. The disciples are anxious and worried at the beginning of this passage. What does Jesus say solves their anxiety?

How does hope of eternity with Christ change your current anxiety?

Record Your Thoughts

Prayer: Thank You, Father, for the words of Jesus which tell me to trust in You when I am anxious and troubled. I am anxious. I want to trust You. Help me trust. Amen.

Power Prayer for Week 5: Thank You for Your truth which conquers my fears.

Day 2

One of the first projects I start young people with is pajama pants. For pajama pants, you sew each leg first: the outer seam and the inner seam. Then, you connect the two legs at the crotch (or rise seam). To do this, turn one leg inside out, while the other leg is right side out. Place one leg inside the other leg, lining up the crotch seam. All you see is one leg of the pants inside out. It never fails that the students get a baffled look on their faces wondering how this backwards, inside out pant leg will ever turn into pajamas.

Sometimes when we look at the events of the world, we may want to look at God and freak out, wondering how this mess could turn into the beauty that He promised. The plan doesn't seem right, and we question whether God messed up.

Let's start with what we say we believe, according to the Bible. Matthew 24 says that there will be wars, famine, and earthquakes in the last days. These things are hard to endure. As we see them happening in our world, dwelling on them will completely ruin any peace that we have. It is only natural to be concerned about our lives.

Turn your thoughts back to week 1, when we discussed attaching to God as your good Father. The foundation of trust that we build with Him is so imperative to our approach to all the hardship that we see in the world.

We can mourn with those who mourn and grieve our own losses as well, but God has already told us His plan. We can know with confidence that eternity with Him forever will be glorious, because there will be no more pain or sorrow and we will be with Him forever. For our time on this earth, we are not promised freedom from pain.

There is a point at which you must choose to believe. Do you believe God is trustworthy? Do you believe that He loves you and His plan is perfect? When you see the disasters and pain of this world, you must choose what narrative you will tell yourself. Such as, "The world is such an awful place. I fear what the future will bring." Alternatively, you can say, "I believe God is at work, carrying out His plan. I choose to stay close to Him and trust Him even in hard times."

Read: Matthew 24:6-13, "You will hear of wars and rumors of wars, but see to it that you are not alarmed. Such things must happen, but the end is still to come. Nation will rise against nation, and kingdom against king-dom. There will be famines and earthquakes in various places. All these are the beginning of birth pains.

Then you will be handed over to be persecuted and put to death, and you will be hated by all nations because of me. At that time many will turn away from the faith and will betray and hate each other, and many false prophets will appear and deceive many people. Because of the increase of wickedness, the love of most will grow cold, but the one who stands firm to the end will be saved."

Optional Additional Reading: Revelation 21:1-4

Reflect: What events of the world cause you to feel anxious or worried? In light of these Scriptures, how do challenging events relate to God's eternal plan?

Record Your Thoughts

Prayer: Lord, there are many terrible things happening in the world today. If I focus on them, I feel anxious. I believe that this is part of what You said would happen. I trust You are good and that You are with me each day. Amen.

Power Prayer for Week 5: Thank You for Your truth which conquers my fears.

Day 3

Claire Hunte writes, "Cloth holds onto its material memory. Cotton will stubbornly retain the mark of its folds in the faintest of lines that no amount of ironing can fully erase."[12] As I left my full-time job to become a stay-at-home mother and sewing entrepreneur, the fear of financial ruin was constantly with me. I thought I had worked through my issues of trusting God, yet like others who have experienced financial hardship as children, I was like the cotton retaining the faint lines of my past.

Our past shapes our beliefs. But as adults, we must grow up and do the work to train our hearts and minds in faith.

I realized if I wanted to experience God's peace, I had to teach myself His absolute truth which is superior to my perceived experience of truth. Some of my biggest questions was, "Does God provide?" and "Will He provide for me?" From the limited perceptive of my experience, I believed that God had let me down in these areas during my childhood. These were the questions I had to answer in order to move forward with God.

Through this I began learning how imperative it is that we teach our minds and hearts God's truth above our experience. Though I have come so far, the memories still return, and I fight the battle of renewing my thoughts once again. Scripture always serves as the best source for learning about His provision. The passage telling of His provision for the Israelites as they walked through the wilderness for 40 years has been especially meaningful to me. Did you know that in Deuteronomy 29:5 it says that their clothes and sandals did not wear out for these forty years?! I have been a seamstress for a long time. Most of the items clients bring for repair are less than 10 years old. Shoes and clothing are important, and they cost money to replace. Not only did God provide bread from heaven in a proactive way, He also provided by preserving what they already had.

There have been many times when I prayed, "Lord, You preserved the clothing and shoes for the Israelites. I believe you will preserve the clothing and shoes of my family as well." Shoes and clothes for three growing kids were expensive and often not in my monthly budget. Time and again, God provided. As I experienced His faithfulness, my faith grew. Believing God provides starts with the willingness and tenacity to keep our focus on Him and what His word says is true, not on the surrounding circumstances or on the memories of our past.

Read: Deuteronomy 29:2-6, "Moses summoned all the Israelites and said to them:

Your eyes have seen all that the Lord did in Egypt to Pharaoh, to all his officials and to all his land. With your own eyes you saw those great trials, those signs and great wonders. But to this day the Lord has not given you a mind that understands or eyes that see or ears that hear. Yet the Lord says, "During the forty years that I led you through the wilderness, your clothes did not wear out, nor did the sandals on your feet. You ate no bread and drank no wine or other fermented drink. I did this so that you might know that I am the Lord your God."

Optional Additional Reading: Deuteronomy 29

Reflect: What provisions does Moses remind the people about in this passage? What provisions of the past did God give you?

Record Your Thoughts

Prayer: Thank you, Father, for my mind to understand, my eyes to see and my ears to hear the provision that You have made for me in the past. I trust You to continue to provide today, tomorrow and for the rest of my life. Amen.

Power Prayer for Week 5: Thank You for Your truth which conquers my fears.

Day 4

Until recently, I wasn't aware of how distinctly different an in-person business is versus an online business. Technology is amazing! I love meeting people via Zoom and social media. But I simply cannot pin fit a dress exactly unless you are right in front of me. Granted, several times I have had Zoom consultations with clients and friends (especially during the COVID-19 pandemic) trying to walk them through the steps of how to measure the alterations. The results weren't terrible, but nothing compares to the benefits of having a dress on the client right in front of me.

God doesn't need to meet us via Zoom. He isn't in a different state or time zone. He is here with us. Yet, how often we act and feel like He is not. Let's look at some Scriptures about God's presence. These verses are taken from the ESV:

Psalm 16:11, "You make known to me the path of life; in your presence there is fullness of joy; at your right hand are pleasures forevermore."

Psalm 139:7-8, "Where shall I go from your spirit? Or where shall I flee from your presence? If I ascend to heaven, you are there! If I make my bed in Sheol, you are there!"

These two passages alone speak of the closeness of His presence. In other passages, He reminds us not to be afraid because He is with us and will help us. The book of James exhorts us to draw near to God, and He will draw near to us. Personally, I have experienced a lack of peace because I feel like He isn't near, or I feel abandoned. In part, this has been because of my experience as a child and the feelings of abandonment that I felt when my father died. However, we cannot allow the narrative of our feelings to become our belief and still expect to encounter the peace of God. When feelings tell us a reality other than God's truth, we must do the hard work of processing the feelings.

Processing the feelings involve recognizing them. Then we must teach them truth. I have prayed something like this, "God, I feel abandoned now. Even as a child I felt abandoned when my father died. But I know I live in an imperfect world and that death is a result of sin from the beginning. I want to believe like the psalmist that You have not abandoned me and I cannot go anywhere outside of Your reach. I want to draw close to You and experience the peace of Your Presence. Amen."

The sample prayer is an example of acknowledging the feeling, but turning to God with a teachable heart, choosing to believe that He is the Father who will never abandon you just as He said.

Read: James 4: 6-8, "But he gives us more grace. That is why Scripture says: 'God opposes the proud but shows favor to the humble.' Submit yourselves, then, to God. Resist the devil, and he will flee from you. Come near to God and he will come near to you. Wash your hands, you sinners, and purify your hearts, you double-minded."

Reflect: Have you ever considered yourself to be proud when you elevate your feelings above God's truth? In what ways can you submit your feelings to God (not bury them or hide them, but submit them)? What are some practical ways you can draw near to God when your feelings are telling you He is far away?

Record Your Thoughts

Prayer: Father, thank You that You are near me and You see me each moment of my life. I want to live close to you and be continually aware of Your Presence. Help me prioritize my thoughts to dwell in Your Presence. Amen.

Power Prayer for Week 5: Thank You for Your truth which conquers my fears.

Day 5

As I stood in my studio, chatting with a client about the last de-
tails of her project, my two-year-old was walking around the room with
a yardstick in his hand. She nervously glanced at him, and asked, "Aren't
you afraid that he will hurt himself with that?" The question took me by
surprise. I've always known that having sewing supplies in the home could
pose a potential threat to young kids, though certainly the yardstick posed
a much lower risk than pins and scissors.

Fear of what could happen can keep us from moving forward into
what God calls us to do. The core teachings of our faith teach us that God
is the protector of the righteous. Read the accounts of Daniel and the lions'
den, David and Goliath, and Queen Esther, and you will see God as a mirac-
ulous protector. It's true that we all ask the question, "What about the bad
things that happen to 'good' people?"

We have pain, and we experience loss and hardship. Yet, deep
within your soul, you must settle the question: Do you believe God is your
protector?

When we experience tragedy, hard questions are normal. We can
bury them or choose to face them. God is not afraid of our questions or our
desire to find answers. I don't know all the reasons that God allows these
things to happen, though I know we are still in a battle of good and evil in
the spiritual realm and the battle is not yet over. I know and believe that in
the end, God has the victory.

Our questions do not anger God. In our questioning, He wants us
to press in to seek Him, draw close to Him, and fix our gaze completely on Him. Personally, I have found that when I look around me at what is
happening, I can get overwhelmed and fearful. But when I look to Him and
confess my belief in His word, the fears fall away.

When I think of protection, I am also reminded of the Israelites in
Exodus 11 & 12. At this time, they were in slavery in Egypt. God had brought
a series of plagues upon Pharoah for refusing to let the people go free.
The Israelites were instructed to sacrifice a young lamb and smear some of
the blood on the doorframes of their houses. This blood on the doorposts
protected the Israelite households when God passed through and killed the
firstborn of every Egyptian family in the final plague. What if the Israelites
only believed with a mental assent that God was powerful but did not act
on His instructions? Their firstborn sons would not have been protected.

In a similar way, we have been given the gift of Jesus, who shed His perfect blood for us. He also symbolizes the Passover Lamb. Do you believe that His blood also protects you and that His word is true? Do you believe He gives direction and wisdom that will keep You safe?

Read: Exodus 12:12-13, "On that same night I will pass through Egypt and strike down every firstborn of both people and animals, and I will bring judgment on all the gods of Egypt. I am the Lord. he blood will be a sign for you on the houses where you are, and when I see the blood, I will pass over you. No destructive plague will touch you when I strike Egypt."

Optional Additional Reading: Exodus 12

Reflect: What are your thoughts about God's protection? Do you believe He protects you? What are some reasons you struggle to believe in His protection?

Record Your Thoughts

Prayer: Lord, I believe You are my protector, just as you protected the Israelites from the death of their firstborn son. As I continually place my trust in You, believing in the power of Christ's sacrifice on the cross for me, may I know and experience Your protection. Amen.

Power Prayer for Week 5: Thank You for Your truth which conquers my fears.

Day 6

I think of belief and trust as the stitches that hold our faith together. To become a better sewist, I must observe the areas that need work. I may need to try a different technique or type of thread. Other times I've had to learn which needles work best in a fabric or become aware of how fast to push the machine on a project like leather.

Webster's 1828 dictionary points out that the root of the word "faith" is the Latin word "fides" or "fido," which means "to trust." The expanded definition of faith (among many others) is "belief; the assent of the mind to the truth of what is declared by another, resting on his authority and veracity without evidence."[13]

This week, we have covered belief and trust in God's plan, provision, presence, and protection. This belief and trust wrapped together is faith. Hebrews 11:6 says that without faith, it is impossible to please God. Faith engages the mind and body.

With my sewing business, I had to learn to apply my belief about God and the truth of His Word to my business. Rather than listen to my negative thought patterns, I used journaling, spoken thoughts, and prayers to renew my mind. This in an example of my prayers: "Lord, I believe that You have called me to do this. I believe You are good, and Your love endures forever. I trust that You will show Your goodness in my everyday life." Rather than looking at your fears, you are responsible for speaking truth over yourself, your business, and your household.

Throughout this devotional, I have been writing power prayers for you. These prayers are affirmations of belief you must teach your mind so the teachings of the Bible will penetrate your body, will, mind, and soul. You need to form your own power prayers, based on Scripture, so that belief and trust grow out of your whole being, not just out of an intellectual theology.

As I read the testimony of saints of old from Hebrews 11, I am reminded that they were people just like me. When I put myself in their shoes, I know their faith was strong enough to stand when they couldn't see the outcome. I want to be like them. I hope you do as well.

Read: Hebrews 11:5-8, "By faith Enoch was taken from this life, so that he did not experience death: 'He could not be found, because God had taken him away.' For before he was taken, he was commended as one who pleased God. And without faith it is impossible to please God, because anyone who comes to him must believe that he exists and that he rewards those who earnestly seek him. By faith Noah, when warned about things not yet seen, in holy fear built an ark to save his family. By his faith he condemned the world and became heir of the righteousness that is in keeping with faith.

By faith Abraham, when called to go to a place he would later receive as his inheritance, obeyed and went, even though he did not know where he was going."

Optional Additional Reading: Hebrews 11

Reflect: What do you think of the long list of men and women counted as righteous? If you were to place yourself in the shoes of these individuals, what feelings or emotions do you think they overcame to walk in faith?

Record Your Thoughts

Prayer: Thank You Father, that by faith, You will help me hold on to and believe Your truth, rather than focusing on my fears. Amen.

Power Prayer for Week 5: Thank You for Your truth which conquers my fears.

Week 6: All the Parts Working Together

Thank You for making all the parts of my being work together in peace.

Day 1

One fall, the local farm stand asked if I could repair their outdoor market tents. It was my slow season for the sewing business, so I agreed. These tents were bulky and dirty. Toward the end of the pile, my industrial machine gave me trouble. I kept breaking needles for no apparent reason. After I completed the tents, I continued to have trouble with my machine. Sometimes the thread would break. At other times, the needle would break. I couldn't figure out the exact problem until I called my friend who runs a sewing machine repair shop.

As I explained the trouble, she asked a series of questions.

- Was the throat plate rough? (That's where the needle goes down.)
- What about the bobbin casing?
- Was it smooth?
- When I turned the handwheel and watched the needle move up and down, did the needle hit any place underneath?

There were issues with some parts of my machine, which created a problem with my stitching.

Our sinful nature is like the sewing machine. The signs of trouble are there. It could be sleepless nights, angry outbursts, pits in our stomach, a gnawing sense of anxiety, an inability to be present, or a variety of other things. But do you know what is wrong?

Let's face it—when something is wrong, you are not at peace. I've come to recognize the signs of trouble with my sewing machine and trouble with my heart. When I notice frequent anger in my tone, a restless anxiety, and a general darkness over my mind, I come to God asking Him to show me the root. Sometimes it is a negative thought triggered by a recent situation. Other times it is a new season that worries me. There is a myriad of reasons for my feelings, and it takes time to process them in His presence.

Stitching peace into your journey means learning how the parts of your being work together to create secure stitches that will create a lasting piece (peace).

Read: Colossians 3:15, "Let the peace of Christ rule in your hearts, since as members of one body you were called to peace. And be thankful."

Reflect: When you sit in silence, do you feel at peace with yourself? Reflect over the past few days, and jot down situations in which you noticed you were worried or anxious.

Record Your Thoughts

Prayer: Father, I long for peace in Your presence. I believe it is Your will for me to live at peace. Amen.

Power Prayer for Week 6: Thank You for making all the parts of my being work together in peace.

Day 2

The sewing machine comprises so many parts. As mentioned yesterday, the motor of the sewing machine was fine, but there were slight damages or misalignments in a variety of other pieces. My understanding of my sewing machine challenges is that while I was stitching the tents, the weight of them created a strong tension or drag on the needle, which caused the needle to get pulled off-center.

As I was stitching, the needle descended into the throat plate slightly off-target, which caused the needle to hit the shuttle, which held the bobbin case and broke the needle. When the needles repeatedly hit the shuttle, the needle came back up through the throat plate bent, which caused burrs in the metal of both the shuttle and the throat plate. Then, as the needle went back down again, it would break.

While I was stitching at a significant speed, the broken needle sometimes got stuck in the bobbin case and shuttle while in motion, which jarred the position of the bed shafts that controlled the motion of the machine. The broken needle would occasionally jam in the bobbin case and shuttle while the machine was in motion, which led to a disruption in the timing and halted sewing until these issues resolved.

It wasn't just one incident that was the problem with the machine—it was many, which contributed to the malfunction. Just as it is never truly one thing that causes the lack of peace in our souls, often it is many things.

But what exactly is this soul that longs for peace with God? In his book "Soul Keeping," John Ortberg relates a conversation he had with Dallas Willard. Dallas explained to him he was not merely a self, but a soul—a soul created by God and for God, designed to rely on God and not meant for self-sufficiency. He said that it is not our external circumstances, thoughts, intentions and feelings that run our life, but it is our soul. By his account, the soul is the part of our whole that correlates, integrates, and enlivens all the rest of what we call ourselves.[14]

Since you are reading this devotional, I assume you desire to live at peace. This has to do with a flourishing inner life of peace regardless of external events. Repairing, maintaining, and caring for the broken, stressed, and buried parts of ourselves is necessary to find peace in our souls. The other parts addressed in the book "Soul Keeping" are the will, mind, and body. This book was pivotal in my journey toward peace, as I understood how all these parts work together to create the inner life flowing from the soul.

The soul is also the part of us that connects to God. Think back to week one of this devotional: how the crux of Christianity is that we must securely connect to God as our Father. When the soul lacks peace, connection is hard. Often throughout the Scripture, the word heart is used to describe soul such as in this passage.

Read: Ephesians 3:14-21, "For this reason I kneel before the Father, from whom every family in heaven and on earth derives its name. I pray that out of his glorious riches he may strengthen you with power through his Spirit in your inner being, so that Christ may dwell in your hearts through faith. And I pray that you, being rooted and established in love, may have power, together with all the Lord's holy people, to grasp how wide and long and high and deep is the love of Christ, and to know this love that surpasses knowledge—that you may be filled to the measure of all the fullness of God.

Now to him who is able to do immeasurably more than all we ask or imagine, according to his power that is at work within us, to him be glory in the church and in Christ Jesus throughout all generations, for ever and ever! Amen."

Reflect: Where is Christ making his home in you? In what ways has your soul experienced the love of God? Do you feel a lack of experiential love of God?

Record Your Thoughts

Prayer: Father, thank You for empowering me by Your Spirit and filling my soul with Your love. I desire to establish a strong, indwelling connection with Your Spirit in order to stitch myself in Your love. Amen.

Power Prayer for Week 6: Thank You for making all the parts of my being work together in peace.

Day 3

I pulled out the next project and sat down at the machine, turned on the motor, placed the fabric under the presser foot, and pushed the foot pedal. Two stitches forward led to a dead stop. The needle snapped and became entangled in the shuttle, bobbin, and throat plate. I worked to dislodge the broken needle and restarted the machine. This time I wouldn't be stitching anything; the shuttle had twisted on the bed shaft and the timing of the machine was off enough that the needle hit the shuttle as it came through the throat plate.

In a moment, as I realized my project had halted, a flood of thoughts consumed me. "I will not meet my deadline. I won't get paid for the job. We won't be able to pay the mortgage."

Thoughts are like that. We are triggered, and suddenly we can be over our head in anxiety. I had sat down in this chair to sew thousands of times before. There was no conscious thinking involved in starting up the machine to stitch a project because I had lots of experience. In a similar way, the experiences of lack and poverty that had influenced a personal narrative within me. I didn't purposefully go down the thought path which led to anxiety; it was an automatic reaction.

Throughout the day, we think a lot of thoughts—50,000 to 70,000. Most of the time, we are actively thinking at least seven thoughts at a time, along with many unconscious, automatic thoughts. As I gained awareness of my own reactions, I became fascinated with thought pathways, triggers, and how they relate to the tapestry of my life that I am stitching. There will be more about thoughts in future weeks, but for now, take some time to reflect on the thoughts that you think. Step back to observe them.

If we renew our minds, Romans 12:2 explains that we will undergo transformation. Strong's Concordance defines the mind in this verse as the God-given capacity of each personal to think and the organ of receiving God's thoughts through faith. The thoughts that come into your mind should not dictate your life. As you reflect on your thoughts, take note of whether they reflect God's truth.

Read: Romans 12: 1-2, "Therefore, I urge you, brothers and sisters, in view of God's mercy, to offer your bodies as a living sacrifice, holy and pleasing to God—this is your true and proper worship. Do not conform to the pattern of this world, but be transformed by the renewing of your mind. Then you will be able to test and approve what God's will is—his good, pleasing and perfect will."

Reflect: Write some of the negative thoughts that went through your mind in the past day. There are Bible verses that speak to most of our feelings or emotions. What does God's word have to say about your thoughts?

Record Your Thoughts

Prayer: Father, I struggle with negative thoughts that just seem to pop into my mind. I want to think Your thoughts about me. Help me recognize the negative thoughts and speak Your truth over them. Amen.

Power Prayer for Week 6: Thank You for making all the parts of my being work together in peace.

Day 4

If only I could make the machine work again by sheer willpower. But we all know it just doesn't work that way. Instead, I must use my will (or decision making) to decide how to best go about fixing the machine. Typically, the first step is to put out an SOS signal to my husband because he is pretty good at fixing things. Over the years he has become proficient at repairing my industrial machine.

I used to think that conquering anxiety could be accomplished by willpower. After all the verses of Philippians 4, found at the end of today's devotional, are an exhortation to refrain from anxiety. But anxiety does not leave simply by "willing" it away. However, our will can help us to move forward by asking questions. With a sewing machine I think of these as troubleshooting questions such as, "Why did the machine break? What were the warning signs that this was happening? How can I prevent it from happening again?" As I processed through these, I set a boundary. I will not be mending tents again.

In a similar way, when anxiety comes you can activate your will to troubleshoot the issues. Ask questions about the nature of your feelings. When did they start? What action would ease the anxiety? Are there people or situations surrounding the feeling of anxiety? As you repeat this troubleshooting process over time, you will learn more about yourself, your personality, your family and your past.

Engaging in this type of questioning activates your will, which is a choice. When thoughts come into your mind or when you are tempted to do something you know isn't good for you, you can make a choice. Sometimes, though, thoughts become jumbled in your mind, causing you to feel you can't think straight because emotions are involved. This leads to a paralysis of the will, which equals an inability to decide. This confusion is a stark contrast to the peace of God we long for in our lives.

Rather than allowing our will to be directed by every random thought that comes into the mind, the will needs to be the keeper of the mind. The easy road is to allow thoughts to be on autopilot, without expending the energy to process and redirect them. We need to actively take part in deciding what thoughts to keep and which ones are toxic.

Read: Philippians 4: 6-9, "Do not be anxious about anything, but in every situation, by prayer and petition, with thanksgiving, present your requests to God. And the peace of God, which transcends all understanding, will guard your hearts and your minds in Christ Jesus.

Finally, brothers and sisters, whatever is true, whatever is noble, whatever is right, whatever is pure, whatever is lovely, whatever is admirable—if anything is excellent or praiseworthy—think about such things. Whatever you have learned or received or heard from me, or seen in me—put it into practice. And the God of peace will be with you."

Reflect: What actions in these verses are a choice? What would it look like for your own life to choose thoughts that align with these principles? Take a few moments to look back at your notes from this verse in week 3.

Record Your Thoughts

Prayer: Father, I desire to pray about all things rather than being anxious, but sometimes I forget. I ask for help that I would hear the prompting of the Spirit, who reminds me to turn to You in prayer when I am anxious. Amen.

Power Prayer for Week 6: Thank You for making all the parts of my being work together in peace.

Day 5

Outwardly, this ordeal had done no damage to my machine. It remained fixed to its table, resting in the oil pan, and attached to its powerful motor. But while damaged, it could no longer perform its intended function. It was out of action.

We've reviewed the soul, mind and will. Now let's look at the body. I think of the body as the action. Several passages in the Bible use the action word "walk." Walk by the Spirit (Galatians 5:16), walk in the light (1 John 1:7), walk worthy of your calling (Ephesians 4). Walking is purposefully putting one foot in front of the other to head in a certain direction with a planned course.

In our spiritual lives, our goal or destination is to connect our soul to God and to continue to form that strong attachment for the rest of our lives. When your mind, will, and body are walking according to God's truth, you will arrive at your destination of connecting in a deeper way with God.

There are actions we take with our body that impact our physical health, which also affects the other parts of us (mind, will, and soul). Some of these could be dietary, which could affect our feelings and emotions. For example, some people have a higher sensitivity to sugar and will feel symptoms of depression when consuming too much. Another action that we take with our bodies is physical activity, through which the body releases endorphins. These endorphins also combat feelings of depression.

Other actions such as gambling, fornication, and filthy language also keep us from experiencing peace. God created you to be a vessel of His glory, radiating the person of Christ within you. Your body should be treated with respect as a dwelling place of the Living God.

Recognize that what you do with your physical body affects your inner life of peace and your ability to walk out your life of peace with God. Dietary and lifestyle changes can be habits, which will take time to break. Accountability or community with others who are also working on the same thing can help you stick with the changes you are trying to make. As you put in the work necessary to make these changes, stay focused on the goal of secure attachment and ask God to teach you His wisdom in these areas.

Read: Galatians 5:19-26, "The acts of the flesh are obvious: sexual immorality, impurity and debauchery; idolatry and witchcraft; hatred, discord, jealousy, fits of rage, selfish ambition, dissensions, factions and envy; drunkenness, orgies, and the like. I warn you, as I did before, that those who live like this will not inherit the kingdom of God.

But the fruit of the Spirit is love, joy, peace, forbearance, kindness, goodness, faithfulness, gentleness and self-control. Against such things there is no law. Those who belong to Christ Jesus have crucified the flesh with its passions and desires. Since we live by the Spirit, let us keep in step with the Spirit. Let us not become conceited, provoking and envying each other."

Reflect: Jot down the actions of the flesh listed in verse 19-21. Can you relate to any of these actions? What actions do verses 25-26 list? Which actions will build on your connection to God?

Record Your Thoughts

Prayer: Father, thank You for the willpower to choose the actions that I do with my body. From eating habits to exercise habits to moral actions, I want to walk in step with Your Spirit in all that I do. Thank You for sending the Holy Spirit as my helper in all these things. Amen.

Power Prayer for Week 6: Thank You for making all the parts of my being work together in peace.

Day 6

Over the years, I've learned a lot about my sewing machines, including how they work and how to care for them. Most of the learning has come from mistakes I have made, often because I pushed them too hard. So much of the process of sewing is about making sure all the parts of the machine are working properly and allowing all the moving pieces to work together in harmony. I have learned to recognize warning signs, especially when the motor makes a certain sound or an unusual clack occurs.

As you gain understanding about the workings of your inner person—your responses, emotions, will, and functions—you can notice the warning signs that all is not well within. Rather than just being an anxious person, you too can learn to care for yourself and cultivate a more peaceful life.

This week we have only touched the surface, but awareness is the first step to progress. As we stay focused on the goal of the Christian life, which is to connect with God, then our words, thoughts, and actions will reflect this connection as well. That is what it's like to live with an integrated soul; all the parts of our being are working together to lean towards truth and wholeness in Christ.

Think about the great commandment to love God with all your heart, soul, mind, and strength. In his commentary of Matthew 22:37, Matthew Henry wrote we must unite our hearts to love God, as opposed to having a divided heart.[15] I have often considered the commands in the Bible as duties, but they actually guide us towards a life of fulfillment. When all our parts unite and work together to love God, peace comes to our hearts and souls.

In contrast, the divided heart is never peaceful. Rather than seeing these commands of the Bible as duties, receive them as messages of His love and care for you. He knows what is best—what will bring peace and what will not. Caring for yourself is a joy and a privilege that will bring forth peace in your life.

Read: Matthew 22:37, "Jesus replied: 'Love the Lord your God with all your heart and with all your soul and with all your mind.'"

Reflect: This week, what are some important points about your will, mind, and body integrating into your soul?

Record Your Thoughts

Prayer: Lord, I desire to love You with all my heart, soul, mind, and strength. Often, I fail to focus my attention. Help me continually shift my gaze and direction back to You and Your truth as I strengthen my relationship with You. Amen.

Power Prayer for Week 6: Thank You for making all the parts of my being work together in peace.

Week 7: Tangled Threads

*Thank You for teaching my mind Your truth
and setting me free from my negative thoughts.*

Day 1

Dozens of spools of thread with corresponding bobbins fill my shop. For a while I tried to organize them on a rack, but the loose ends of the bobbins and threads always became entangled. They created a cluster of interwoven threads that looked more like an impossible knot than functional thread for productively stitching projects together.

This picture of thread reminds me of the toxic memory trees that Dr. Caroline Leaf writes about in "Who Switched Off My Brain?" and the image of bad thoughts she shares in the book.[16] Over the past decade, I have spent countless hours reading books on the mind, brain, and emotions. My reading and research have predominantly been for my journey because I was desperate to change my own mental narrative. One could classify this determination as willpower. But for this week we will be working to untangle the knotted mess of threads, called our thoughts. As they are untangled, they will be put to work to create beautiful, stitched creations for the rest of our lives.

You've already spent time several weeks ago processing belief and trust. Dr. Timothy Jennings writes that "when we believe lies about God, those false beliefs actually damage us, change our neural circuits and warp our minds and characters."[17]

Bad thoughts, negative self-talk, and toxic thinking certainly do not cultivate an inner life of peace. Messages of positive thinking saturate our culture, proclaiming that it fixes our thought lives. But just thinking about something pleasant or successful that isn't rooted in the truth about God will not help you have true peace in your heart. Instead, just as Dr. Jennings wrote, we must reframe our thinking based on what God says is true. This will bring about a peaceful heart.

This week you will work to untangle those threads of thought and belief that crowd your mind with tangled knots. As you engage in this work, remember all you have learned so far in this devotional. God, your Father, loves you so much! He does not intend this to be hard work. Instead, the words of Matthew 11:28-30 are an invitation, "Come to me, all you who are weary and burdened, and I will give you rest. Take my yoke upon you and learn from me, for I am gentle and humble in heart, and you will find rest for your souls. For my yoke is easy and my burden is light."

Read: 1 Corinthians 14:33, " For God is not a God of disorder but of peace— as in all the congregations of the Lord's people." (Though the context of this verse is within the church, I believe that God's will is also that we are free from internal confusion.)

Reflect: What are some thoughts that feel jumbled in your mind?

Record Your Thoughts

Prayer: Lord, I desire to believe what is true. I want to focus my thoughts on a true belief in Your character. Help me recognize what false beliefs I have about You. I believe You desire for my mind to be free from confusion. Amen.

Power Prayer for Week 7: Thank You for teaching my mind Your truth and setting me free from my negative thoughts.

Day 2

For sewists who only sew occasionally, often they have a grandmother's machine and an old sewing box. It's a big frustration when they get out the machine and start stitching only to have the thread repeatedly break. Did you know that even though you inherited your grandmother's sewing kit, it's recommended to ditch the thread in it? Thread stored in the attic for decade will be more brittle, because it has experienced moisture, humidity, and fluctuating temperatures.

It appears this sewist has all the tools for success, but the thread holds back progress. Immediately, this brings on a mindset of failure. Perhaps the narrative runs something like this: "I'm a failure. I've failed God. I have not been able to complete my task, and I should just give up."

Truth: The thread is simply old and brittle.

Failure is a common negative mindset. What do we believe about God when we fail?

For starters, let us remember God is a God of persistence and perseverance, and failure in our eyes does not mean failure in His eyes. Failure could be part of a trial that is part of the refining process God has for you.

When we focus on failure instead of seeking strength from God, we become defeated and forget God's plan is about His Kingdom's purposes being fulfilled on earth, just as they are in heaven. One of His main purposes is for us to be transformed into the image of Christ. This will involve our refining.

Thinking that the world is all about our success or failure means our inner peace can change from moment to moment, depending on what the day's accomplishments look like. Just as old thread breaks when you sew, the mindset of failure also prevents you from troubleshooting the problem.

Dr. Leaf also points out that having an unrealistic expectation of your own performance puts your mind and body in stress mode, which negatively affects your health.[18] When you feel failure, readjust your expectations and ask God to show You His purposes in your situation. He wants to use this for the kingdom purpose of transforming you. Expect His transformation. Don't give up. He will never give up on you.

Read: James 1:3-8, "because you know that the testing of your faith pro-duces perseverance. Let perseverance finish its work so that you may be mature and complete, not lacking anything. If any of you lacks wisdom, you should ask God, who gives generously to all without finding fault, and it will be given to you. But when you ask, you must believe and not doubt, because the one who doubts is like a wave of the sea, blown and tossed by the wind. That person should not expect to receive anything from the Lord. Such a person is double-minded and unstable in all they do."

Reflect: When do you have thoughts of failure? Write your thoughts. How do your thoughts correspond to God's truth?

Record Your Thoughts

Prayer: Father, thank You I don't have to be perfect. Thank You for the persistence to know when to keep going even when I feel like I am doing it all wrong. As I persist, I ask You for wisdom in the situation, believing that You delight in giving wisdom to Your children. Amen.

Power Prayer for Week 7: Thank You for teaching my mind Your truth and setting me free from my negative thoughts.

Day 3

Scrolling through social media, I see the gowns, slipcovers, and other sewing projects that sewing entrepreneurs have created. Their pictures look perfect. When I look at my work, I feel I'm not good enough. Quickly I can fall into a foul mood, believing that I just don't have enough skills to offer sewing services to the community.

No matter how far we progress, the thought "You aren't good enough" can impact the memory trees of our brain. It's likely a thought you've had before, so it is a familiar pathway. The danger of familiarity is that it feels safe and comfortable, so you offer it hospitality without attention to its toxicity. Before long, it is playing on eternal repeat as it circles in a basal ganglia loop.

This thought must be stopped; however, telling yourself that you are good enough is not the solution. Let's get straight to the biblical truth. As unpleasant and curt as it may sound, you simply aren't good enough. All fall short of the glory of God (Romans 3:23). This simple truth should bring our pride to a screeching halt.

The biblical law is humility. Compared to the perfection of Christ, you are not good enough. Why does that sound so bad? Why do we feel the need to pit ourselves against someone else in comparison, wanting to be better than them? There will always be people to whom we want to compare ourselves, as if our value comes from our outward appearance or actions.

You don't have to be good enough. God never asks that of you. Instead, He affirms that you are loved. In fact, He tells us to highlight our weaknesses, so we can tell of His power. I am not a highly trained tailor, but God blessed my business. He gave me mentors and patient clients along the way who helped me hone my skill.

Whatever insecurities you have, let God use you just as you are and see what He will do. Rather, than trying to compare yourself to others, humbly embrace the person He has created you to be. You don't need to outshine someone else in your field, family, or community. You are His, and He delights in you. Let your weakness be an opportunity for Him to be glorified.

Read: 2 Corinthians 12:9, "But he said to me, 'My grace is sufficient for you, for my power is made perfect in weakness.' Therefore I will boast all the more gladly about my weaknesses, so that Christ's power may rest on me."

Ephesians 1:4-9, "For he chose us in him before the creation of the world to be holy and blameless in his sight. In love he predestined us for adoption to sonship through Jesus Christ, in accordance with his pleasure and will—to the praise of his glorious grace, which he has freely given us in the One he loves. In him we have redemption through his blood, the forgiveness of sins, in accordance with the riches of God's grace that he lavished on us. With all wisdom and understanding, he made known to us the mystery of his will according to his good pleasure, which he purposed in Christ."

Reflect: In what areas have you struggled with thinking you are not good enough?

Record Your Thoughts

Prayer: Thank you, Lord, that in You, I don't have to be enough. You gave Your Son for me and I believe, as Your word says, it brings You pleasure to bring me into Your family. Thank You for promising that Your power will be perfect in my weakness. Amen.

Power Prayer for Week 7: Thank You for teaching my mind Your truth and setting me free from my negative thoughts.

Day 4

I glanced down at my phone to see a voice text from a number I didn't recognize. It looked suspicious, and with all the spam calls these days, I wondered if I should even open it. Curiosity got the best of me, and I listened to the message.

It wasn't spam. Instead, it was a newly engaged bride who needed alterations for her wedding gown. But she wasn't even in my area. In the voice text she told me how she had been praying about a seamstress for her gown and she felt like God kept impressing her with the name "Naomi." She searched her whole area to find a Naomi that sewed but couldn't find one. Then she went to call a friend and saw my name "Naomi-seamstress" in her contacts. More than six years earlier she lived in New York and had brought me a bridesmaid dress to alter but had totally forgotten. She didn't even know why she was calling since I lived so far away, but she felt God so strongly impress my name on her spirit.

I was able to direct her to some bridal alteration specialists in her area, but this voice text was far more meaningful to me. For weeks I had been groaning to God about my workload, asking whether this was what He called me to do or if I needed to be writing more. This message was God saying, "I see you. I know what you do for work, and I will bring you the people I intend for you to meet. Every part of your life is holy, including your work."

All I wanted was to know from my heart that He sees me. He sees the sewing, the raising kids, and the writing. He sees.

Genesis tells the account of Hagar who struggled with feeling unseen. She was a servant to Abram's wife Sarai. Sarai could not bear children. In her impatience for a child she told her husband Abram to have sex with Hagar, hoping Hagar would conceive an heir. After the act was done, Sarai was jealous and mistreated Hagar. In response, Hagar ran away. God met Hagar while she was in the wilderness. He saw her pain and gave her a promise that she was already pregnant with a child. From this encounter, Hagar called God the God who sees.

We all want to be seen, heard, and valued. In the secular world, this results in a great deal of family and workplace conflict. The messages of culture tell us we deserve to be heard, listened to, and seen. This causes us to focus on our needs, wants, and desires more than on God or someone else. Being seen is a deep, human need. To be seen by our Perfect Father in heaven brings peace, even though recognition and being seen by others is a wonderful thing.

Our feelings and emotions play a huge part in our outlook. Feeling unseen can cause you to tell yourself the false narrative that you aren't valuable. With the rising statistics of suicide rates, clearly this is a false narrative that is running rampant throughout our culture.

The truth of God's Word, His promises, His character, and His Spirit give you the opportunity to train your mind, will, and emotions in the true narrative. Your worth is immeasurable. You are seen. You are loved.

Read: Genesis 16:13, "She gave this name to the LORD who spoke to her: 'You are the God who sees me,' for she said, 'I have now seen the One who sees me.'"

Optional Additional Reading: Genesis 16

Reflect: In what areas do you feel unseen? What do you need to talk about with God regarding this?

Record Your Thoughts

Prayer: Father, sometimes I struggle with feelings of insignificance. I want to be seen, heard, and valued. Yet, when I think of Jesus, who men rejected, I am reminded that being seen by others is not important. Instead, I am so thankful to know that You see me and You value me. Thank You! I love You, Lord. Amen.

Power Prayer for Week 7: Thank You for teaching my mind Your truth and setting me free from my negative thoughts.

Day 5

"My sewing machine hates me."

I've heard it so many times. Just yesterday, as I was teaching a lesson on one of those highly computerized sewing machines, it kept beeping and flashing red. The manual stated that the beeping and flashing red indicate improper threading. Sure enough, when we re-threaded the machine, it worked perfectly.

It's so easy to place the blame, isn't it? Perhaps it's the sewing machine you feel like is against you, or perhaps it's God. If you have experienced a series of disappointments, setbacks, traumatic events, etc., you may be tempted to believe that God is working against you. As much as you don't like to hear it, the problem is never with God, but with us. Just like the sewing machine that just needed to be re-threaded, we often just need a perspective reset.

Many of our actions and decisions are based on our internal state —whether we feel confident, afraid, insecure, worthless, etc. For example, if you already feel worthless, you are more likely to choose a life partner who does not build you up. This can lead to a challenging life. God isn't against you, but you may have acted out of your own feelings about who you are rather than who God says you are.

The cycle of poor choices is often rooted in low self-esteem and our chronic, self-defeating actions. This also causes us to expect failure in the things we set out to do. The only solution to this is drawing near to Christ and asking Him to teach us about the love of the Father. The more we know who God has made us to be, the closer we get in relationship to Christ. As we know His love and acceptance, the more emotionally, mentally, and spiritually mature we become. This allows us to make thoughts and decisions based in God's reality.

God is for you, not against you. Let Him burn this truth on your heart. This path is the path of peace.

Read: Romans 8:31-39, "What, then, shall we say in response to these things? If God is for us, who can be against us? He who did not spare his own Son, but gave him up for us all—how will he not also, along with him, graciously give us all things? Who will bring any charge against those whom God has chosen? It is God who justifies. Who then is the one who condemns? No one. Christ Jesus who died—more than that, who was raised to life—is at the right hand of God and is also interceding for us. Who shall separate us from the love of Christ? Shall trouble or hardship or persecution or famine or nakedness or danger or sword? As it is written:

'For your sake we face death all day long; we are considered as sheep to be slaughtered.'"

No, in all these things we are more than conquerors through him who loved us. For I am convinced that neither death nor life, neither angels nor demons, neither the present nor the future, nor any powers, neither height nor depth, nor anything else in all creation, will be able to separate us from the love of God that is in Christ Jesus our Lord."

Reflect: In what ways do you feel like God is against you or that you have hit a brick wall? What does this passage say about God?

Record Your Thoughts

Prayer: Thank You, Lord, that You are for me. Thank You that You sent Your own Son for me, so that I can experience Your love and favor. With my mouth and my heart, I confess and believe that You are for me. Amen.

Power Prayer for Week 7: Thank You for teaching my mind Your truth and setting me free from my negative thoughts.

Day 6

Lack of organization for spools of thread can result in them tangling together or unraveling, which creates quite a mess! The thread needs to be untangled before it can be used for sewing. In the same way, while our minds are a cobweb of tangled thoughts and emotions, we can't walk out the purpose God created for us, which is peace and fellowship with Him. These thoughts must be untangled.

Recall the quote at the beginning of this chapter from Dr. Timothy Jennings, "when we believe lies about God those false beliefs actually damage us, change our neural circuits and warp our minds and characters."[19] These lies that we believe about God often creep into our thoughts through circumstance, experience, and the words of others.

The four specific lies that we covered this week are "I'm a failure," "I'm not good enough," "no one sees me," and "God is against me." Each of these thoughts contains false beliefs about God. God doesn't see you as a failure; instead, He encourages persistence. God doesn't ask you to be good enough, because He already knows that in your own strength, you are nothing. Yet, He still calls you a beloved, chosen son or daughter. It's true that not everyone sees you, but God sees you and that is all that matters. God is for you, not against you—nothing can separate you from His love.

If negative thoughts have been long entrenched in our minds, it will take some time to correct the neural pathways. Your thoughts will automatically want to go down the familiar, toxic path. As you recognize the false beliefs for what they are and choose to combat them with a truth about God, your brain will form healthy thought processes, which in the long term will bring you inner peace. The primary way to learn the truth of God's character is through reading Scripture. The accounts of His interactions with people in the Bible give insight into His character. Just like we studied Hagar—God saw her, and He sees you. Spend time with God reading the Scripture on a regular basis and ask Him continually to reveal to you how it applies to your life.

Read: Psalm 139:23-24, "Search me, God, and know my heart; test me and know my anxious thoughts. See if there is any offensive way in me, and lead me in the way everlasting."

Reflect: Take a moment to consider: when you are thinking any of these negative thoughts, do you feel at peace, or do you experience a greater level of anxiety? While you focus on these false beliefs about God, what emotions are you feeling?

Record Your Thoughts

Prayer: Lord, search my heart. Show me my anxious thoughts. I want to walk in Your everlasting way. I want to believe what is true about You. Help me recognize false beliefs in my thoughts immediately and teach me the truth about You. Amen.

Power Prayer for Week 7: Thank You for teaching my mind Your truth and setting me free from my negative thoughts.

Week 8: Overwhelm Steals Peace

Thank You for providing rest for my soul.

Day 1

This past fall as our new homeschool year began, I quickly felt over-whelmed and anxious with the pressures of business and the schooling of three kids. During this summer, I had been quite flexible with client sched-uling and had done a bit of sewing work during the morning hours. Howev-er, the school year demanded new work hours. Figuring out how to juggle extracurricular activities, the homeschool co-op schedule, field trips, sewing time, client appointments and meal planning felt like an advanced round of Tetris. It all left me with feelings of overwhelm and anxiety, which were quite the opposite of a peaceful heart.

Overwhelm is not new to God's people. I love the account of Moses' overwhelm in Exodus 33. He was leading hundreds of thousands of people to an unknown place. (Meanwhile, I am only leading three young people and a business—just to put it in perspective.) I can only imagine that Moses had way too much to do and the responsibility he carried was something he struggled with sometimes. In Exodus 33, Moses was concerned about who God was going to send with Him to help with the people. When he cried out to God, God reassured him, saying, "I will go with you and give you rest." (Exodus 33:14)

Perhaps the promise that God is always with us is one that you have heard repetitively. But the concept of God giving rest is not so familiar. Both because of our culture and the natural human bent to validate the meaning of our existence, rest is not something toward which we gravitate.

When we look at our tasks, thinking they are our primary responsi-bility, then we will immediately feel overwhelmed. But to follow the example of Moses crying out to God and hearing His answer, we can trust He is with us and will give us rest. However, if we are not near Him, we will not be in proximity to receive His rest, or to even hear His voice offering it. When you feel overwhelmed, cry out to Him. He hears you and longs to reveal His faithfulness to you. He may give rest by showing you what to take off your agenda, or He may give rest through the strength found in His presence.

Read: Exodus 33:12-14, "Moses said to the Lord, 'You have been telling me, "Lead these people," but you have not let me know whom you will send with me. You have said, "I know you by name and you have found favor with me." if you are pleased with me, teach me your ways so I may know you and continue to find favor with you. Remember that this nation is your people.'

The Lord replied, 'My Presence will go with you, and I will give you rest.'"

Optional Additional Reading: Exodus 33

Reflect: What does God's promise of rest mean to you?

Do you feel:

overwhelmed

weary

burnt out

(circle one or all)

Do you think that peace within is possible when you don't feel rested?

Record Your Thoughts

Prayer: Lord, I am [overwhelmed, weary, burnt out (insert your own)]. I want to experience the rest that You promised Moses. I know that I have a lot on my plate, but I am not the exception, as I see Moses had far more responsibility than I do. I believe that living from a place of rest is Your plan for me. Amen.

Power Prayer for Week 8: Thank You for providing rest for my soul.

Day 2

The mother's voice on the other end begged, "I just found the perfect dress for my daughter's prom, but it is a little too big. Can you alter it for us? Her prom is on Saturday. I know it's the last minute, but could you just get us in for an appointment today?"

I love helping people. It's one of the most satisfying aspects of my work. But feeling pressured by other people's last-minute shopping is not part of the deal. I used to listen to all the excuses about why they didn't have the dress earlier. Sometimes I would cave in and agree to take the job. Without fail, I would feel the emotions of their emergency transfer onto me, as I rushed to finish an ill-fitting dress perfectly in a matter of 48 hours.

Hurry steals peace. There is a time and place for the unexpected, such as suit pants for a funeral, but if we live life as an emergency, we will never enter God's peace. When I feel the sense of emergency rise, I think of Ann Voskamp's words: "Calm. Haste makes waste. Life is not an emergency. Life is brief and it is fleeting but it is not an emergency."[20]

Jesus was pressured by all the demands of needy people that He loved. Yet, He took time to be with people. Perhaps as I turn down emergency client jobs, it may look like I am not taking the time for people. However, it is always important to remember that saying yes to one thing most often requires saying no to something else. Living life as an emergency is a common lifestyle in modern America. There are so many facets to this: over commitment, lack of boundaries, and unrealistic expectations. No longer is there the necessary margin to hear or to be.

Over the years, I have learned to walk out the type of life that I want to live by creating boundaries around my time and schedule. Life is not an emergency. Hurry is the opposite of rest. Most often, it leaves me feeling like I'm wrestling with time rather than living within it. Twenty-four hours in a day are gifts. Learn to live within the boundaries of time as God intended.

Read: Psalm 46:10, "He says, 'Be still, and know that I am God; I will be exalted among the nations, I will be exalted in the earth.'"

Reflect: What activities, projects, or commitments in your life cause pressure for you? In what way do these line up with what you value?

Record Your Thoughts

Prayer: Father, I dislike the feeling of anxiety that comes with hurry. I want to work with you to cultivate a peaceful heart. Help me prune away excess busyness. Amen.

Power Prayer for Week 8: Thank You for providing rest for my soul.

Day 3

When sewing, you never want to sew too close to the edge of the fabric. If you do sew too close to the edge, the seams will come apart after minimal wear. It makes for an unstable garment, pillow, quilt, or slipcover. This is called seam allowance. For example, manufactured sewing patterns have a standard seam allowance of 5/8 inch, intending for the needle to be stitching five-eighths of an inch from the edge of the fabric.

On the throat plate of most sewing machines, there are markings for 1/4, 1/2, and 5/8 inch seam allowances. These are a guide so that as the fabric passes under the presser foot, you can also focus on the seam allowance throughout the project. Often the attention of a novice sewist will drift, and before they know it, the seam allowance is much too large or small. It takes some practice to master the hand eye coordination necessary for guiding the fabric and operating the machine.

Seam allowance is like margin. With too little, the unraveling will begin. Think back to week one. The goal of our faith is to form a secure attachment to our Father. This brings peace. Textiles fall apart without enough seam allowance. Without margin, you don't have the time or space to care for your own soul, which is your connection to God, to yourself, and to others.

You may start off with good intentions of what your priorities are and even a plan for how to keep those. But as opportunities arise and life happens, your attention can quickly get diverted. Before you realize it, you are overcommitted, and all margin is gone. Like the coordination and focus needed to master sewing a straight line with proper seam allowance, it will take time to learn the art of creating and maintaining margin.

In recent years I have begun using the Google calendar app in my phone to keep track of appointments, clients, church, and all the activities. Because the Google calendar has time slots, it provides me with a visual representation of white space between activities. As I have gotten to know my personality and the rhythms of healthy connection with God and family, I have developed an awareness of how much white space I need on the calendar to live unhurried. Holding margin has become a form of maintaining a rhythm of rest in my life. It doesn't mean a life without productivity, but involves recognizing the amount of margin necessary for my soul to thrive. Margin in my life is not perfect; it is a continual work in progress.

Read: Psalm 37:3-6, "Trust in the Lord and do good; dwell in the land and enjoy safe pasture. Take delight in the Lord, and he will give you the desires of your heart. Commit your way to the Lord trust in him and he will do this: He will make your righteous reward shine like the dawn, your vindication like the noonday sun."

Reflect: How much margin do you feel you have in your life? What does margin look like for you? Look at your answers to yesterday's questions. Are they things you must do, or can you prune some of them out of your life? You may fear that margin means cutting a bunch of things out of your life, but personally, I think it is much better to refine your margin a bit at a time over years. Eventually, margin will become a habit.

Record Your Thoughts

Prayer: Lord, I want to have more margin in my life, but sometimes I just don't know where to begin. Please grant me the wisdom and strength to know where to implement margin. Amen.

Power Prayer for Week 8: Thank You for providing rest for my soul.

Day 4

Over the years, I have had the most unusual project requests: a cloth amoeba-like creature for a larger-than-life display, specialized pants for skateboarding, motorcycle tire warmers, and a stuffed goblin shark, among many others. Unique projects caught my attention because I love the creativity and challenge that goes into each of them. However, I found that these types of projects detract from my ability to stay focused on my primary client base. This distracted focus left an undercurrent of anxiety. I had to take time to decide what the purpose of my sewing business was.

Before going further, let me point out that not all anxiety is bad. We all feel a little anxious when starting something new that we haven't done before. Doing new and scary things can be an area in which God is stretching us. However, you need to spend time with God to discern what He is leading you to do and what His purpose for you is.

My spiritual dad, Walt, used to remind me that the One who called me is faithful and He will do the work, which is a paraphrase from 1 Thessalonians 5:24. He would remind me not to fear moving toward what God called me to do, because God would be faithful in that. Rather than living in fear of walking outside His will, I ask Him to show Himself faithful in the areas on which He wants me to concentrate.

You aren't called to be a doer of everything. Being a performer is a natural inclination for many of us. Doing all the good things is not the pathway to peace. You don't have the capacity for that. This concept applies to all areas of life, from raising your children to extended family commitments, level of church involvement and work-related commitments. Start with asking: "What am I called to do?" It may take some time to find the answer to this. Reflect on the things at which you are naturally talented. I have a hard time looking inward to recognize my gifts, but have found it helpful to ask those closest to me what they see as a gifting or talent in my life.

Additionally, you can reflect on what experiences or work you have done that made you feel most alive. This also maybe a clue to understanding God's purpose for your life. Ultimately only God can show you the specifics of what He has called you to do. Remember the first and most important thing He has called you to is a transformative relationship with His Son, Jesus.

Read: Ephesians 2:8-10, "For it is by grace you have been saved, through faith—and this is not from yourselves, it is the gift of God—not by works, so that no one can boast. For we are God's handiwork, created in Christ Jesus to do good works, which God prepared in advance for us to do."

Reflect: What does Ephesians 2:10 say about what He created you to do? Throughout this week, you have been observing the activities in which you are involved. Take some time to sort them into categories.

Record Your Thoughts

Prayer: Father, thank You for creating me with purpose. I believe that You already have good work planned for me to do. However, I get distracted by all the things which keep me too busy. Help me recognize and choose the things that You have called me to do and give me the courage to say no to the rest. Amen.

Power Prayer for Week 8: Thank You for providing rest for my soul.

Day 5

Yesterday, I mentioned the variety of projects that people have asked me to do over the years. At first, I took some of them. After a while I recognized the pattern of what type of projects brought me life. I purposefully set a boundary, resolving that I would not take design projects, clothing from scratch, or prototype manufacturing. When requests come now, I already have an answer. I've done the mental work of determining that isn't something I will do, so the "no" comes naturally.

Setting the boundary, or the standard, is one of the first steps to conquering the overwhelm. My example is for business. If you are not self-employed, you have less control over work decisions. But work is only a fraction of our lives, and these types of boundaries apply to every aspect of activity and involvement.

Boundaries start by taking to meet with God, and objectively thinking about what He would like your life to look like. If you have a healthy marriage, it would be beneficial to work on this with your spouse as well. These are some sample questions to consider. How much time do I want to or need to dedicate to work? How many days a week do I want to eat together as a family? What extra commitments should I be taking on? What relationships, such as marriage and friendships, do I need to invest in?

I've also noticed that lack of boundaries can sometimes be rooted in pride. I have said "yes" to commitments because I wanted to be the one to jump in to save the day. I wanted to be known as the one on whom everyone could call. Perhaps you see this in yourself as well.

As you process through your schedule, it is not a time to turn your life upside down by canceling everything. Learning boundaries is a slow process that may take months or years to cultivate. Even in the middle of the overwhelm, copping out of a commitment is not the answer because that will tempt you to believe that you are a failure and you are unreliable, which will only exacerbate mental stress. Instead, finish the commitment and make the decision now to not sign up again once it's completed.

Boundaries with time cultivates a healthy respect for God's gift of a 24-hour day. Trust Him to make the most effective use of your time for His Kingdom.

Read: James 4:13-15, "Now listen, you who say, 'Today or tomorrow we will go to this or that city, spend a year there, carry on business and make money.' Why, you do not even know what will happen tomorrow. What is your life? You are a mist that appears for a little while and then vanishes. Instead, you ought to say, 'If it is the Lord's will, we will live and do this or that.'"

Reflect: Pray over the areas of your life where you feel overwhelmed and ask God to show you how that relates to the verses you just read. Six months from now, what type of boundaries would you like to see in your schedule? What things would you have to let go of to get there?

Record Your Thoughts

Prayer: Lord, I have so many things to do. I want to live with more boundaries so that I reduce overwhelm and walk more fully in Your peace. Help me cultivate these. Thank You for the wisdom that You give. Amen.

Power Prayer for Week 8: Thank You for providing rest for my soul.

Day 6

Earlier this month, I received a text message from someone with whom I had not previously worked. A few weeks prior, she had contacted me about slipcovers, which is one of my specialties, but then she had never responded. The new text was a request about adding lining to some fabric she had already hung as curtain panels. This request came in January, which is my slower season. I convinced myself that I could use the work even though this is specifically on my "no" boundary list.

Later that evening, I confessed to my husband that I was already feeling overwhelmed by the thought of doing these. I messed up. I said yes when I wanted to say no and everything in me was feeling the anxiety of that decision. It may feel silly, but our souls feel the effect of the boundaries that we cross. Decisions don't just affect one aspect of our lives; they affect our being from the inside out.

Along comes the grace of God. The lady never followed through with the curtains. She never dropped them off. Now, I was free to decline the work because she didn't bring them in during my time frame anyway. When I cry out to God in my overwhelm, talking to Him about the stress that I face in all areas, He is faithful to work in the situation. I believe that as we live in a relationship with God our Father, connected to Him in communication and love, He works on our behalf. Often it is a matter of trusting Him. Rather than thinking of Him as a judgmental Father who is driving us to achieve works for His kingdom, He longs for us to draw near in an attitude on communion and conversation with Him.

As you do the work to slow your hurry, increase your margin, focus on your calling, and set boundaries, peace will fill your heart. But there will be times your peace will be disturbed by unexpected events or by your own lack of boundaries. Don't stress. It happens to all of us. Take a deep breath, say a prayer, give it to God, and trust that He can work it out.

Read: Proverbs 3:5-6, "Trust in the Lord with all your heart and lean not on your own understanding; in all your ways submit to him, and he will make your paths straight."

Reflect: Continue to review your schedule, commitments, boundaries, and margins. Follow the example of the Scripture you just read in Proverbs 3. Consider implementing a routine practice of committing your plans and responsibilities to the Lord each day.

Record Your Thoughts

Prayer: Lord, I believe that when I work with You to create boundaries in my life around the purpose for which You have uniquely designed me, You will direct my path, even when I mess up. Thank You. Amen.

Power Prayer for Week 8: Thank You for providing rest for my soul.

Week 9: Identity Impacts Peace

Thank You for calling me Your beloved child.

Day 1

I am a sewing professional. It took more than a decade in business before I could embrace the title. I didn't feel worthy of the title. I didn't have a background in fashion design and had no degree behind my name to prove that I could do the work. Additionally, I felt guilt about not operating the way that many other businesses do. I've always had a home studio, which seemed less professional than colleagues who have a store front. These identity issues are commonly referred to as imposter syndrome and affect the level of confidence we project in our work, family, and relationships.

Lack of self-esteem and confidence attributes to lack of peace. When you accept Christ as your Savior, you become a child of God—loved, chosen, accepted, holy, set apart, and forgiven. Yet, if you are anything like me, you don't always feel you can embrace this identity. You think you aren't worthy of the title. Perhaps you feel you are a Christian imposter. Maybe it is a sketchy past, family history, hidden scandals, or insecurity that keeps you from believing you can take on the identity God tells us we have.

Not only does God say all these wonderful things about us, but He also says each of us is uniquely designed for His purpose. I knew the Scriptures about God designing me for His purpose, but I thought the only purpose valuable to God was Christian ministry. I struggled to believe that the creativity of sewing was part of my unique design. The theology of unique design was an abstract truth that lived in my head but was not impacting my heart. I felt worthless for the kingdom because I thought I was letting God down, rather than embracing the gifts He gave.

This week, you will delve into these aspects of identity and explore how they affect a peaceful life. Lack of identity can be dangerous for our souls because we all long for validation. We want someone to tell us who we are, and that we have worth and meaning in the world. If we do not fix our hearts heavenward for validation, then we will restlessly wander through life. We will crave the affirmation of those around us, which will only leave us hopeless and empty. Instead let us find identity and security in our relationship with God. As you do, you will find who He created you to be.

Read: Psalm 63:1-4, "You, God, are my God, earnestly I seek you; I thirst for you, my whole being longs for you, in a dry and parched land where there is no water. I have seen you in the sanctuary and beheld your power and your glory. Because your love is better than life, my lips will glorify you. I will praise you as long as I live, and in your name I will lift up my hands."

Reflect: When you think of yourself, who are you? List some words that immediately come to mind. Don't think of good words that you know you should write. Think about the words that you speak over yourself in your mind.

Do the words you speak over yourself make you want to search for God and the value He speaks over you?

In what way could you compare the identity you speak of yourself to a parched and weary land?

Record Your Thoughts

Prayer: God, I believe You call me loved, chosen, forgiven and so much more. These are not the words I call myself, but I want to take on the identity of who You say that I am. I earnestly thirst for You to be present in my mind and in my body. Amen.

Power Prayer for Week 9: Thank You for calling me Your beloved child.

Day 2

  If we aren't careful, the mistakes that we make contribute to the narrative we tell ourselves. Whether it be sewing or the events of our lives, when we speak, we are telling our version of the story to ourselves and to others. The sewing story you speak may be, "I can't sew a straight line." This is a story without context and is a blanket statement of failure. What if the same story went like this: "When I was 12 years old, I sewed a pillowcase in home economics class. I had never operated a sewing machine before and needed some work on my hand-eye coordination, so my stitching was wobbly. My best friend's mom was a tailor, and her pillowcase turned out almost perfectly. She laughed when I showed her mine and told me I'd better leave the sewing to professionals. I never tried to sew again, and just assumed I didn't have the skill."

  The first version of the story takes on the identity of inability: "I am a failure. I am not a sewist." This narrative keeps you from trying. When we unbury the complete story, we can make peace with history. The simple facts are that you were new to sewing. You weren't an instant success (who is anyway?). People laughed at you. You felt ashamed. However, none of these truly have anything to do with your identity. They are just simply an experience you have had that may give you challenges in the process of sewing success.

  Pain, heartache, failures, abuse, and childhood trauma fill our pasts with stories. But these stories are not your identity. They have shaped your personality and perspective of both life and of God. But you can learn to tell your story differently.

  In some circumstances, the story is so painful that we don't know how to tell it. You may need to sit with a counselor or trusted friend, or you may need to process through it by journaling. When all we can say about our stories is that we can't or that we are a failure, we will not experience the peace God offers when our identity is shaped by Christ. We also cannot move into the potential He has planned for us. This disconnect creates in the soul a sort of cognitive dissonance that does not embody peace. As you invite Your Father into your story, He will give you the understanding and healing needed to make peace with your past and tell a new narrative.

Read: Luke 4:16-21, "He went to Nazareth, where he had been brought up, and on the Sabbath day he went into the synagogue, as was his custom. He stood up to read, and the scroll of the prophet Isaiah was handed to him. Unrolling it, he found the place where it is written:

'The Spirit of the Lord is on me, because he has anointed me to proclaim good news to the poor. He has sent me to proclaim freedom for the prisoners and recovery of sight for the blind, to set the oppressed free, to proclaim the year of the Lord's favor.'

Then he rolled up the scroll, gave it back to the attendant and sat down. The eyes of everyone in the synagogue were fastened on him. He began by saying to them, 'Today this scripture is fulfilled in your hearing.'"

Reflect: What Old Testament passage did Jesus come to fulfill? List some things listed in this passage about the work Jesus would do. Luke 4:18 in the KJV specifically says, "heal the brokenhearted." Are there ways in which "brokenhearted" would describe the identity you have taken from your story?

Record Your Thoughts

Prayer: Lord, I experienced brokenness and shame, and... (list whatever fits your story), but I believe You sent Jesus to heal and restore me, so that I could live healed from my story. Help me take the time to acknowledge and process the events of my life. I welcome You into my story, as You change it and fill me with peace. Amen.

Power Prayer for Week 9: Thank You for calling me Your beloved child.

Day 3

As I kneeled to pin the hem of a dress of this mother of the bride, an image flashed through my mind. Jesus kneeled to wash the feet of the disciples. He kneeled as an act of service. Here I was kneeling on the floor to serve. I was doing something for a client she couldn't do herself.

Back in week 4, you reflected on the example of Jesus—how He was a servant to others and serving is a way to walk in peace. To take it one step further, serving needs to become part of our identity. The voice of culture tells us we need to become someone, continue to grow a platform, scale our business, and come out on top. Growth and influence are good, but what is the main purpose of our lives?

Jesus knew who He was. In Philippians 2, it says that He emptied Himself and took on the form of a servant. Perhaps you wonder how it is possible to take on the identity of daughter (or son) of the King and the identity of servant. If we truly ponder the role of a king, His job is to serve the needs of the people with wisdom and authority. Jesus as the Son of God in human form, living on the earth, served with authority and wisdom. He knew when it would be beneficial to heal and speak and when it would be beneficial to refrain.

For years I felt like I was restlessly chasing something, trying to be someone and do something. That's what we do when we aren't secure in our identity. My spiritual dad taught me so much about being available and present as a form of service. One of the greatest human needs is to be seen. Others want to know that you see them and hear what they have to say. In week 7 we talked about our own need to be seen by God. As He heals our hearts, showing us the ways that He sees us, He also gives us the responsibility of serving others by seeing them.

With the advances of cell phone technology in the past ten years I have found it even more challenging to maintain a posture of presence and service because of the distraction of the phones. When you are with others, think about the ways that you can serve them with your presence and attention.

Read: Philippians 2:3-11, "Do nothing out of selfish ambition or vain conceit. Rather, in humility value others above yourselves, not looking to your own interests but each of you to the interests of the others. In your relationships with one another, have the same mindset as Christ Jesus: Who, being in very nature God, did not consider equality with God something to be used to his own advantage; rather, he made himself nothing by taking the very nature of a servant, being made in human likeness. And being found in appearance as a man, he humbled himself by becoming obedient to death—even death on a cross! Therefore God exalted him to the highest place and gave him the name that is above every name that at the name of Jesus every knee should bow, in heaven and on earth and under the earth, and every tongue acknowledge that Jesus Christ is Lord, to the glory of God the Father."

Reflect: Who have you been called to serve? (Pray about this and ask God to show you.) Are you content with the identity of a servant? In what ways do you see authority and wisdom going along with servanthood?

Record Your Thoughts

Prayer: Father, often I restlessly try to become someone. In my hurry, I forget to think of serving others. I want to have the attitude that Christ had—to be a servant to those around me. Amen.

Power Prayer for Week 9: Thank You for calling me Your beloved child.

Day 4

Starting a sewing business wasn't Plan A or Plan B on my list during my adolescence. I had always liked to sew, but I had never seen it as a valuable skill set for a business. As I mentioned earlier this week I struggled to embrace the title of professional seamstress. During the early years of business, I would feel guilty for charging money for simple mending, such as patching a hole or sewing on a button.

My identity was, "I am just a seamstress," with the innuendo that I was not a lawyer, a doctor, a teacher, or a college-educated professional. Just a seamstress seemed like simple, unimportant work with my hands.

As part of the body of Christ, how often do we belittle the significance of what we offer, though God gives us those very gifts to offer? Subconsciously, we look around to see those in positions of leadership, musical gifting, and full-time ministry, and we think they have more to offer than we do. We are "just the church members." We allow this comparison trap to take away our peace and contentment with the life that we've been given to live. Rather than pressing into God to find out how He wants to use the gifts, we have we are restless, insecure, and always looking to do the next thing to prove our value.

I've been there. My plan A was full-time ministry. I didn't have a Plan B or C or D. When that plan didn't work out, it crushed my identity. Sitting behind a sewing machine is a far cry from overseas mission work. But my spiritual dad kept challenging me to ask God for the opportunities where I am. Many of those opportunities have not been in the limelight of church leadership. Yet through the past fifteen years, God has implanted in me identity about my place in the body of Christ and it is valuable.

The same is true for you. He has given you unique gifts, talents, and abilities. If you release any preconceived notions about what it means to serve Him, you'll be amazed at how life unfolds. Seek Him. Listen to His voice. He says you are valuable.

Read: 1 Corinthians 12:21-27, "The eye can't say to the hand, 'I don't need you!' The head can't say to the feet, 'I don't need you!' In fact, it is just the opposite. The parts of the body that seem to be weaker are the ones we can't do without. The parts that we think are less important we treat with special honor. The private parts aren't shown. But they are treated with special care. The parts that can be shown don't need special care. But God has put together all the parts of the body. And he has given more honor to the parts that didn't have any. In that way, the parts of the body will not take sides. All of them will take care of one another. If one part suffers, every part suffers with it. If one part is honored, every part shares in its joy.

You are the body of Christ. Each one of you is a part of it."

Reflect: Do you feel you have value and purpose in your life? In what areas do you struggle to feel valuable? How can you reframe the verses of 1 Corinthians 12:21-27 to speak life and value over yourself?

Record Your Thoughts

Prayer: Father, thank You for giving me gifts, talents, and abilities that are an asset to Your Kingdom work on earth. Sometimes I don't see what my talents are. I ask for the eyes to see and the heart to believe. In Jesus' name, Amen.

Power Prayer for Week 9: Thank You for calling me Your beloved child.

Day 5

The garment begins as a length of fabric spread out on the cutting table. The pattern pieces are pinned on and carefully cut to size. As the pieces get sewn together, they are no longer just a piece of fabric. It is a garment held together by tiny, individual stitches.

Perhaps we are a bit like the yardage of fabric. Yet, when we let God in, He creates a beautiful masterpiece. This reminds me of Isaiah 64 verse 8: He is the potter, and we are the clay. He forms us with His hands. The identity here lies in this—He is the Creator, and we are the created. As He sews the yardage of fabric together, it takes on a new identity. Similarly, as He shapes us, we also take on a new identity.

I am created. You are created not just by chance, but with beauty and skill by the master of the trade. He took time, effort, and forethought into making you unique for a special purpose. The identity of "created" involves sacrifice of control on our part. This could be called yielding or surrender.

But what exactly are we surrendering to become? In Genesis, God tells us that he made man in his own image. Portions of the New Testament refer to us as being transformed and conformed to the image of Christ.

One of my favorite quotes from C.S. Lewis reiterates this by writing, "The more we let God take us over, the more truly ourselves we become—because He made us. He invented us. He invented all the different people that you and I were intended to be. . .It is when I turn to Christ, when I give up myself to His personality, that I first begin to have a real personality of my own."[21]

This underscores the importance of surrendering to the Creator so that He can give us our real personality. While I was wrestling through my past, attachment, and insecurities, I didn't have a real personality. I didn't really know who I was. There was no peace in that state. Instead, it was more like gloomy shadows. But the more I developed that secure attachment to God, the more alive I have felt myself becoming. He longs to make you alive as well.

Read: Ephesians 4:24, "And to put on the new self, created to be like God in true righteousness and holiness."

Reflect: What comes to mind when you think of surrender? In what ways have you seen God shape you, or in what ways to you want to see Him shape you?

Record Your Thoughts

Prayer: Father, thank You for being the Creator. Thank You for the beautiful work that You have done in my life and will continue to do. I want to be transformed into the likeness of Your son. Help me to be cooperative with Your process. Amen.

Power Prayer for Week 9: Thank You for calling me Your beloved child.

Day 6

Perhaps it is maturity that has grown in me to settle into the identity of sewist—to find a joy and contentment in the title. Time has been my friend as I have settled into that identity. No longer restless and in search of meaning, I've learned to tell a new narrative. This home sewing business has been successful because it served its intended purpose by enabling me to be home and present with my children. Along the way, I've also embraced the identity of servant, created, and valuable (along with many others).

This week, as you have sorted through your own narrative, these identities that I've given you to take on may not seem like they fit. The world chases after identity in the form of achievement that elevates self as a creator and master, certainly not as a servant. This may be because we are trying to prove our value to ourselves even more than to the world. Deep inside, we all struggle with the words of accusation that say we are a failure. We want to feel a sense of worth for our existence. Yet, a life of service feels belittling compared to aspirations of being used by God through a large platform. Even in Christian circles the influence of worldly identity creeps in, causing us to think that bigger means we have more value in God's eyes.

All identity which elevates self creates distance from God. Taking on the identity that God gives us is a way of strengthening secure attachment to Him. It could be called coming into alignment with His Word or coming into agreement with Him. In the words of John the Baptist, Christ "must become greater; I must become less" (John 3:30). I think of it as bringing my life and my soul into agreement with what He says about me. I understand why it brings peace to my soul to embrace this identity. When there is agreement, there is peace. Our earthly nature submits to the Spirit. This is peace.

This is a journey of continually shaping our identity. It involves daily asking Him to show us who He created us to be, and who He created us to serve. Though we may not consciously be asking these questions every day, it is more about the bent of our hearts continually leaning into Him to draw our identity from Him.

Read: Galatians 2:20, "I have been crucified with Christ and I no longer live, but Christ lives in me. The life I now live in the body, I live by faith in the Son of God, who loved me and gave himself for me."

Reflect: Look over your notes from this week. How has your perspective changed from the beginning of the week? What steps are you going to take in the future to take on this identity that God has given you?

Record Your Thoughts

Prayer: Father, Thank You for giving me a new identity. I agree with You that this is who I am: You created me with valuable gifts and talents to serve for Your glory. Help me find complete satisfaction, peace, and joy in who you say that I am. Amen.

Power Prayer for Week 9: Thank You for calling me Your beloved child.

Week 10: Troubleshooting Peace

Thank You for the perseverance to continue the journey of peace.

Day 1

One day, I met a former neighbor on the street. She asked how I had been doing, as she hadn't seen me in a while, and inquired if I still had the sewing business. I filled her in on the happenings, assuring her I was still in business and that I was teaching sewing lessons as well. On hearing this, she launched into her own sewing story.

One winter she pulled out her sewing machine, eager to start a project during the gray, northeast winter. But her excitement was short-lived. Before long she had jammed threads wrapped around the bobbin and no finished project to show for the effort. For a while she tried to fix the problems, but eventually became so frustrated that she stormed out on her porch and ditched the sewing machine over the railing into the snowbank. There it stayed until the snow melted. I could hardly contain a chuckle!

The struggle is real! Whether it is understanding your sewing machine, or trying to make peace within your heart, there will be times of frustration. You won't get it right all the time. But now is not the time to give up. You have spent the last nine weeks walking this path to peace with me. Don't stop now. Perhaps you've had setbacks. Maybe it feels like you have more negative thinking than you could ever overcome. You may have had an unnerving encounter with a friend or family member that triggered a buried memory of pain from your past.

There is the temptation to throw it all away - over the railing and into the snowbank, thinking that this will restore peace to your mind. Giving up never brings peace. It only eases the inner tension for a short time. When the snow melts, the problem will still be there, just like the sewing machine. There have been many times when I wanted to give up. Examining my inner life takes a lot of mental effort. Depending on God to teach me and mold me involves surrender, which isn't always pleasant. But when I look back at where I have come from, I see the fruit of peace.

Don't give up now! As you continue working through your thoughts, attitudes, and actions, the journey towards peace will become a habit. The effort is worth it!

Read: Galatians 6:9, "Let us not become weary in doing good, for at the proper time we will reap a harvest if we do not give up."

Reflect: How are you doing on this journey towards peace? What are your areas of frustration?

Record Your Thoughts

Prayer: Father, I'm frustrated. I thought this journey would be easier. Help me to not give up. Thank You for the promise there will be a harvest for the effort I have put in if I do not give up. Amen.

Power Prayer for Week 10: Thank You for the perseverance to continue the journey of peace.

Day 2

I was listening to a sewing podcast this week that interviewed a sewing machine repair specialist. The repair specialist said that often customers will come in with their machines, telling the repair technicians what they think is wrong with their machines, such as, "The tension is off," as if that statement is actually 100% true. Rather than describing the symptoms of the machine to the technician, they have a preconceived notion of the issue.[22] The problems are much easier to diagnose if we name the symptoms such as, there are large loops of loose thread on the bottom side of the stitch. There may be a variety of mechanical issues, but some fixes could be as simple as the need to re-thread the machine.

Too often I hear people say, "I don't have peace," and then tell me how this lack of peace has caused them to make a decision that is more in-line with the will of God. I believe God uses the presence and absence of peace to help us discern His will. But take this peace a step further and name it for what it is. There was one time in my life that I believed God was using lack of peace to tell me something. Most often, He has challenged me to activate my mind, seek counsel, and listen to His direction. This is called wisdom. Rather than make decisions exclusively based on feelings of peace, seek wisdom.

When you must say no to a supervisor because you want to spend more time at home with your family, you probably won't feel a lot of peace. Saying no is hard and uncomfortable. When I put my fingers to the keyboard to post online that I was launching my first book, fear overwhelmed me. I didn't feel any peace at all! I just knew that this was the next step in being obedient to what God called me to do.

Actually, naming with symptoms would be to say, "I am nervous about a conversation I'm going to have with my boss tomorrow. After praying about the decision with my husband for several weeks, I know this is the decision God has shown us. Even though I'm feeling anxious about it, I believe God will give me the courage to speak up." When launching a book, business, or new product, you could say, "I'm doing something new, and it feels a little scary because I don't know what people will think of me."

In both these situations, lack of peace shouldn't give reason to back down. Talk to God about your feelings about the situations in which you lack peace. Ask Him to fill you with the confidence you need to take the next right step. Invite God to give you wisdom on the situation before you act.

Read: Psalm 37:3-5, "Trust in the Lord and do good; dwell in the land and enjoy safe pasture. Take delight in the Lord, and he will give you the desires of your heart. Commit your way to the Lord; trust in him and he will do this."

Reflect: What situation are you in that you don't feel at peace? Write the specifics of why you are feeling anxious about this situation. How can you reframe that anxiety to focus on trusting God with the path He is directing you to take?

Record Your Thoughts

Prayer: Lord, I feel anxious about a certain situation. I have sought You about it and believe You are directing my steps. Thank You for direction. I receive the confidence and courage that You have readily available to me. In Jesus' name. Amen.

Power Prayer for Week 10: Thank You for the perseverance to continue the journey of peace.

Day 3

I was cruising along, in the middle of a project, with the needle rhythmically moving up and down. Suddenly I could feel the tension of the threads as my seam bunched together, and the fabric slowed. "What now?" I thought to myself. "Could it be the bobbin again? Or the thread? Or the needle?" I traced the thread back through the thread guides and realized the thread had become tangled around the spool. Nothing was wrong with the machine. I simply needed to re-thread it.

Some days you wake up and your peace level may seem amazing. Other days, you feel you could just yell at everyone. Before rushing to conclusions about what is wrong, start with the basics. These basics may seem to have nothing to do with your mental health, yet they are just as important to your level of peace with God as your thoughts.

Did you know that the food you eat can affect your mental health (i.e., peace of mind)? I know that too much sugar in my system can cause me to feel irritable and foggy, especially the high concentration that is in birthday cake frosting. I also changed my coffee drinking habits, because I recognized that too much coffee makes me feel jittery. Your body may not respond well to other foods or drinks, as our bodies react differently to foods and sugars. However, it is important to learn how your eating habits may affect your mental health.

The scientific community is conducting more research on the effects of processed food in our diet, which often includes a long list of man-made additives intended to extend the shelf life. I will not teach you about healthy eating in this book, but for further reading on the subject, I recommend "Think and Eat Smart" by Dr. Caroline Leaf. Changing our eating habits, not just as far as dieting to lose weight, but into eating healthier, whole foods, can be challenging. It takes time to learn better foods to eat, and finding where to shop for them can feel overwhelming.

This is something our family has gradually been working on for several years as we have purchased local meats, started growing a garden, and drinking raw milk. Shifting away from food that is "easy" to grab off the grocery store shelf takes some self-control as well. I haven't arrived at perfection in this area, and you may not immediately either. But slow, sure progress is to be commended.

Read: 1 Corinthians 6:19-20, "Do you not know that your bodies are temples of the Holy Spirit, who is in you, whom you have received from God? You are not your own; you were bought at a price. Therefore, honor God with your bodies."

Reflect: Are there certain foods that make you feel you have brain fog? How is your diet overall? What is one thing you could do to make healthier food choices?

Record Your Thoughts

Prayer: Lord, I believe that my body is a temple of the Holy Spirit. You will give me the wisdom and self-control needed to change what needs to be changed in my eating habits.

Power Prayer for Week 10: Thank You for the perseverance to continue the journey of peace.

Day 4

When my spiritual dad passed away, furniture, old clothes, locksmith tools, and more filled his basement to the brim. One day as I worked my way through the basement closet, I stumbled upon a black box about 14" high, 7" wide and 14" across. To my delight, I opened the hinges to reveal a vintage Singer featherweight sewing machine. It is a beauty! But when I took it out of the box to sew, nothing happened. Probably, no one had used it for 30 years, and the lack of movement and oil caused the disrepair. It is totally fixable, just not operational at the moment.

I'm sure I won't be the first one to tell you that lack of movement will cause your body and mind to deteriorate. Physical exercise releases endorphins, which can counteract feelings of depression.

Before kids I had always been active, but after my first baby it was challenging to have any type of schedule. Mostly my exercise comprised of walking to the bank, library, and other errands in our small town while pushing a stroller. I noticed that if I didn't get at least three days of exercise, I would be in a mental funk, out of sorts with the world, grouchy and pessimistic. As the babies grew into toddlers and I became pregnant with my third, pushing the double stroller around town was not an option with upwards of 120 lbs. combined weight and a baby belly. I joined the local gym which had free childcare.

It took years for me to recognize when my anxiety level was tied to lack of exercise. As I began to make this connection, going to the gym or taking a jog were no longer optional activities to partake in "if" I had time. Instead, they became an act of self-discipline. I chose to go because I know I think more clearly, feel happier, and am a better person when I do.

Physical activity does not have to mean a six-day-a-week workout routine. When I first started to implement regular exercise into my life, I thought less than five days a week meant I was a failure. But I had to acknowledge that the purpose of my exercise was for my mental health, not to become a top athlete. Even in exercise when you name the purpose it helps to see the benefits and success. You may feel you don't have the time to exercise. Start small, with little pockets of time. They will add up!

Read: 1 Corinthians 6:19-20, "Do you not know that your bodies are temples of the Holy Spirit, who is in you, whom you have received from God? You are not your own; you were bought at a price. Therefore, honor God with your bodies. (Yes, this is the same verse from yesterday. But such a reminder to care for physical body.)"

Reflect: How much exercise are you getting? If it is not enough, what are some pockets of time you could add a small amount of exercise three days a week? What activity will you do? Note how your mind and body feel afterward.

Record Your Thoughts

Prayer: Father, I want to care for my body through physical exercise, because I believe that You have created my body to rejuvenate through exercise. Help me find an exercise that I enjoy, and that I can also strategically fit into my schedule. Amen.

Power Prayer for Week 10: Thank You for the perseverance to continue the journey of peace.

Day 5

I was almost finished with the slipcover for an overstuffed chair. The fabric was thicker than recommended for a slipcover, but the client was insistent that it would look perfect. The pieces were all stitched together, and now it was time to finish the raw edges. With confidence, I started serging the seams with my Huskylock 905 four thread machine. In some places, where multiple seams came together, the seam was three-quarters of an inch thick. The machine groaned as it tried to go through these thicker portions, but I paid little attention and gunned the foot pedal to the floor. In protest, the machine fell silent, and there was nothing I could do to start it again. A trip to the repair shop confirmed that I had burnt out the motor.

How often I have pushed through life seasons, even though my spirit was groaning. It only leads to burnout of emotions, health, relationships and inner peace. You were not meant to plow through the stress all on your own—just like when I tried to force fat seams through my serger, problems resulted.

Rather than pushing through, we can learn to exercise wisdom. I've learned a few knacks about sewing slipcover seams on my home serger (as opposed to an industrial one). These can also translate into life lessons.

Reflect:

• Thin out the seams by cutting the seam allowance on the piping smaller than the seam allowance of the other pieces. Are there areas of your life that aren't the highest priority which you could trim down?

• Slow down the machine. Slowing down and occasionally manually turning the handwheel when needed makes an enormous difference. How fast are you going daily? In what ways can you take time to slow down?

• Go around the fattest junctions and don't serge them at all. Avoidance is not a recommended tactic for most things. However, sometimes it is okay to preserve yourself and avoid a stressful situation. To know what to avoid, you must first be aware of what the stress point is. Take time for objective observation of stress points.

• Stop. That's right—stop. Simply stop sewing and give the machine a break and pick up the project again tomorrow. Sometimes you just need rest. Listen to your body. Often, when your body is fighting a cold or an illness, a little extra rest at the onset will give you what you need to fight the germs.

Read: Psalm 4:8, "In peace I will lie down and sleep, you alone, Lord, make me dwell in safety."

Record Your Thoughts

Prayer: Thank you, Lord, for showing me where the stressors are in my life. I commit to working with You to deal with them so that I don't burn out. Amen.

Power Prayer for Week 10: Thank You for the perseverance to continue the journey of peace.

Day 6

Troubleshooting these sewing machines is so much about everyday maintenance, such as cleaning, oiling, and threading. When you take care of these things, the rest follows. For some, this everyday maintenance may mean just a slight tweak in daily habits and activities, while for others it may mean a complete lifestyle overhaul.

The work of changing habits and lifestyles is a continual process. This process may seem unrelated to the spiritual goal of connecting with Your Father in a secure attachment. But consider this: a sewing machine can't form firm stitches of connection when it isn't working. When we are hungry, tired, overworked, and lethargic, none of us do well in relationships because we don't have the time or energy. This includes our relationship with God.

Hebrews 12:1-2 encourage us to throw off the things that hinder us and run with perseverance. The peace of God that comes through your secure attachment is the prize you are running toward, and it is worth throwing off habits that get in the way of connecting with Him.

This week we covered so much around habits. Don't change your life all at once. Pick one area per quarter to work on faithfully. Set a realistic goal that you can turn into a habit. These small changes will ultimately direct the course of your life. It has taken years for me to build sustainable rhythms of rest, exercise, and diet that fill my soul with the energy needed to live this full life of homeschooling, running a business, and writing. Several times a year, there are changes in schedules, kids' activities, vacation, and other commitments. These can interrupt the flow of change, and it takes effort both to stay on track and to get back on track.

With small changes over a long period, you can also change your course and live the abundant life that Christ speaks of in John 10:10 as He declares, "I have come that they may have life, and have it to the full." Keep fixing your eyes on Jesus, aiming for the goal of peace within.

Read: Matthew 6:9-11, "This, then, is how you should pray: 'Our Father in heaven, hallowed be your name, our kingdom come, your will be done, on earth as it is in heaven. Give us today our daily bread."

Reflect: What are small habits you could build this year around food, exercise, and rest? Look back over your notes from the week and pick out what stands out to you. Pray over your list, asking God to show you where to start and to help you have realistic expectations.

Record Your Thoughts

Prayer: Lord, sometimes I rush ahead with long lists that I want to change. Thank You for the daily bread of grace, strength, and focus. In my own life, I want to see Your kingdom come and Your will be done as it is in heaven. Amen.

Power Prayer for Week 10: Thank You for the perseverance to continue the journey of peace.

Week 11: Connection To God

Thank You for loving me unconditionally.

Day 1

Deep hues of maroon and gold flowed through my fingers as they passed underneath the presser foot to be joined together by needle and thread. One piece at a time, I connected them to form a custom slipcover for a unique wing chair. It had been challenging to align the fabric around the contours of the arms. This cover could never fit another chair—only this one.

Secure connection is part of the Artist's way of shaping us into the masterpiece we were created to be. Dr. Larry Crabb believed that the primary cause of our struggles is a disconnected soul.[23]   A disconnected soul is not at peace. Instead, peace comes from deep levels of connection to God, your memories, yourself, and others. Over the next two weeks, we will examine what it looks like to have a more connected soul.

Do you feel connected to God? Or is it just a matter of checking off the Christian to-do list? Back in my early 20s, I felt disconnected from God. I didn't know why, as I was in church and reading the Bible. Many verses from the book of Ephesians stirred in me a longing to connect with God in a deeper way. Especially Ephesians 3, when Paul prays that the believers would grow their roots into the love of God. To be rooted is to be connected—drawing all one's nutrients and substance from the Source.

Learning the disciplines of Christianity without connection to the Father is like carefully cutting out all the pieces and never sewing the project together. I want you to desire connection. The beauty of what He wants to create with your life is only possible when you intentionally work with Him to deepen that connection. I am not referring to simply doing the things like Bible reading, group Bible studies, church attendance and serving your church, which are all good things. I'm talking about the desire of your heart to be with Him.

In her book, "Invitation to Solitude and Silence: Experiencing God's Transforming Presence," Ruth Haley Barton shares her journey of learning to truly be with God, compared to being busy for God. When you learn to be with God in silence. you connect with Him and He will make a unique masterpiece with your life.

Read: Psalm 62:5-6, "Yes, my soul, find rest in God; my hope comes from him. Truly he is my rock and my salvation; he is my fortress; I will not be shaken."

Reflect: What do you think of when you think of the "Christian life?" What activities do you associate with "connecting with the Father?"

Record Your Thoughts

Prayer: God, I want that peace that comes from a deep level of connection with You. Thank You that You also desire this for me. I trust You to lead me through the journey as I follow Your Spirit. Amen.

Power Prayer for Week 11: Thank You for loving me unconditionally.

Day 2

I spread out the flannel shirts over the sewing table and tried my best to configure the fronts so I could cut out a large pillow square, with the buttons down the center and the pocket intact. These shirts held the memory of a father, grandfather, brother, husband, and uncle who had recently passed. The family had hired me to make memory pillows out of the shirts. This has not been an uncommon request over the years, as the clothing of a loved one holds their scent, while providing a visual and tactile memory. Having a tangible item to hold and squeeze makes us feel connected to the one who has passed and can be a healthy way to process grief.

When my spiritual dad, Walt, passed away, I felt as if someone had torn me in two. We had talked on the phone almost daily for years. In my head, I knew he was gone, but my heart was not in step with the facts. Grief was the deep pain of severed connection as I unconsciously tried to reach out to the one who was gone, pick up the phone to talk, share a Scripture or a laugh, or simply sit in his presence over a casual lunch.

I had experienced the beauty and joy of a relationship with this man I called Dad. When he was gone, I ached. I knew what I had lost. Adam and Eve had the experience of walking and talking with God. When He removed Himself from that open relationship because of their sin, they felt the loss. Now, thousands of years later, we too feel our hearts reaching out for what once was—to be known, accepted, and connected.

When a loved one passes, sometimes we try to bury the memory by stuffing it down deep where we think we cannot feel it. The grief of loss makes us feel vulnerable, and we know that grief will make us face the fact that they are gone. But hiding the grief away will never bring healing. In the same way, how often do we turn to other things or habits in an effort to bury our souls which are crying out for connection with the Father? Bring the ache to God; He longs to heal that grief.

Read: Psalm 42:1, "As the deer pants for streams of water, so my soul pants for you, my God. My soul thirsts for God, for the living God. When can I go and meet with God?"

Reflect: Do you sense a longing for deeper connection? On a scale of 1 to 10, with 10 being deeply connected and 1 being not very connected, how connected do you feel toward God the Father?

Record Your Thoughts

Prayer: Father God, I long to be with You, to sit in Your presence, and to truly know You and for You to know me. Amen.

Power Prayer for Week 11: Thank You for loving me unconditionally.

Day 3

When you sew, please don't put your foot on the pedal while your fingers are close to the needle. I have heard a few horror stories of trips to the emergency room because a needle went through a finger. Granted, I've been sewing for years, and it has never happened to me. As long as you learn careful sewing techniques, you should be able to avoid this mishap.

Regardless of how uncommon it is for a sewing machine needle to encounter your finger; I've had many beginner students mention how much the needle frightens them. As you guide fabric through the machine, the tendency is to allow your hand to move with the fabric, which brings your fingers closer to the needle. This is where the fear comes in. Yet the needle is necessary for the thread to flow through the fabric to connect the pieces together.

Perhaps on this journey to peace, you are still struggling to connect with God. The relationship is not just about the head knowledge filled with Bible verses and trivia, but about genuine connection. However, fear can be a real factor hindering deep connection. In his book "The God-Shaped Heart," Dr. Timothy Jennings writes about how the most destructive lie that keeps us from knowing God is the beliefs that we hold about God's law, His use of power, and about who He is.[24] Satan is the father of lies and we must recognize that he delights to see these lies take root and affect our connection to God.

Are you wondering why fear matters that much? Consider a child who is afraid of continual punishment. Will that child crawl up on dad's lap for a hug? Probably not, because the child worries about being chastised for some childish act he or she has committed instead of receiving a hug. If you fear God is going to reprimand you every time you get near, you will probably spend more time trying to do things to serve Him than you will actually spend time with Him. Come to Him as Your Father, who loves you. He cares about every worry and concern, and He longs to wrap you in His love.

Read: Psalm 34:8, "Taste and see that the Lord is good; blessed is the one who takes refuge in him."

Reflect: What are your emotions toward God? Do you desire to spend time with Him to know His love? Why or why not?

Record Your Thoughts

Prayer: Thank You, Lord, that You are a good Father. I want to draw close to You to sit in Your love. I choose to believe that You are the loving Father that You say that You are, and I reject the lies of the enemy. Amen.

Power Prayer for Week 11: Thank You for loving me unconditionally.

Day 4

Yesterday I was working on a mother-of-the-groom gown. It needed to be altered from the shoulder seam. This is a simple enough alteration on a sleeveless gown, except in this case the neckline had a yoke, which also had to be adjusted to match the shoulder seam. I carefully removed all the necessary stitches so that the seams would open. As I proceeded with the alteration and began piecing it back together, I needed to cut away some of the excess fabric for it to lay flat. I exhaled for a moment, thinking through the process of the alteration, mentally questioning whether I had done the work correctly. Once I cut the fabric, there would be little room for error. As with all alterations there is a moment of self-doubt, as the voice within my head screams, "What if you ruined the dress?"

Cutting away the excess of our lives can be like cutting away the excess fabric around the alteration. In John 15, Jesus speaks of cutting away branches that aren't producing fruit. In our lives, He is cutting away those fears, emotions, and shame which are not bearing good fruit. It is painful because these have become a part of us. But He wants to take these things away so that we have the energy for producing fruit that reflects the image of Christ. Regardless of how unhealthy the things are that He prunes away, we fear that the pruning might ruin our lives.

This cutting away of the excess is necessary if you want to connect with God and there is the risk of pain. In fact, I would say it will be painful—not because He is a harsh Father, but because an authentic relationship with Him involves transparency. Transparency is like opening the closed seams of the dress, revealing all the raw edges inside. It exposes loose threads to the outside world. Pruning will expose the reality of our past, shame, emotions, fears and so much more to God. He already knows these things, but it is a willingness to surrender that transparency to Him.

Don't let the fear of what God will prune in your transparency keep you from getting close to Him. The benefits outweigh the risk of pain. The promise of pruning is that we will bear the fruit of the Spirit—love, joy, peace, and more. Don't you long to trade your anxiety for peace?

Read: John 15:1-4, "I am the true vine, and my Father is the gardener. He cuts off every branch in me that bears no fruit, while every branch that does bear fruit he prunes so that it will be even more fruitful. You are already clean because of the word I have spoken to you. Remain in me, as I also remain in you. No branch can bear fruit by itself; it must remain in the vine. Neither can you bear fruit unless you remain in me."

Reflect: What has God been pruning in your life? What are you afraid He will prune?

Record Your Thoughts

Prayer: Lord, I'm afraid of what you will prune in my life. But I trust You and know that You are a good Father who desires to fill me with Your love, joy, and peace. I surrender to the process. Amen.

Power Prayer for Week 11: Thank You for loving me unconditionally.

Day 5

The main secret to avoid getting a needle through your finger is to keep your fingers out of the way. Let the machine do the work of pulling the fabric through the machine—that's the purpose of feed dogs. Too often I see novice sewists with their fingers close to the needle trying to pull the fabric through faster than the machine is stitching.

There have been many times when I became impatient with the work of God. Sometimes the impatience concerned my spiritual growth. Other times it was about my work, writing, family, or a myriad of other things. I worked myself into a mental tizzy, trying to figure out how to progress further in these areas. Jada Edwards wrote in the study When You Pray, "In a society obsessively focused on '#goals,' we must modify that to be focused on '#Godsgoals.' His abundant ability is exclusively for His agenda, and we have the privilege of partnering with Him to achieve our portion of it."[25] I have been guilty of focusing on goals for my life and trying to force them to happen, rather than letting God accomplish His goals in me.

I believe that if we stop getting in God's way and let Him do the work, the process would be less painful. He holds the world in His hands. He already knows our fears, shame and emotions anyway, so it isn't as if we can truly hide from Him or fix ourselves without Him.

As you continue reading through John 15, Jesus reveals the secret of a full life. It is to abide in Him. Apart from Him, you can do nothing. If you do not tightly stitch yourself to Him, you can do nothing. Nothing!

Our anxiety levels rise because we get entangled in our own desire to control, but surrendering is the spiritual superpower to connect with God. We need more of Him and less of us. The passage says that when we obey Him, we remain in His love. Envision again that child on the Father's lap, wrapped in His love. He desires you to be in this position. He wants you to be so fully connected to His love that fruit naturally emerges, without requiring a lot of effort from your side.

Your Father loves you—connect with His love.

Read: John 15:5, 9-10, "I am the vine; you are the branches. If you remain in me and I in you, you will bear much fruit; apart from me you can do nothing.

As the Father has loved me, so have I loved you. Now remain in my love. If you keep my commands, you will remain in my love, just as I have kept my Father's commands and remain in his love."

Optional Additional Reading: John 15:5-13

Reflect: Pray and journal about areas that you try to control. What would it look like for you to turn control over to Your Father?

Record Your Thoughts

Prayer: Lord, Your promise of joy and love seems too good to be true. I desperately want my heart and life to be filled with these. Help me surrender control to You continually and allow You to do the work that only You can. Amen.

Power Prayer for Week 11: Thank You for loving me unconditionally.

Day 6

I wrapped up the finishing touches of the maroon and gold slipcover and pulled it over the chair to check my work. I hadn't finished the inside seams with the serger yet, so I knew I might have some minor adjustments to make. Yet, it was close to completion. Creating perfectly fitted slipcovers for unique pieces of furniture is a process. Often, I can only work on one section at a time and frequently bring the work back to the furniture to check the fit.

This work of stitching our connection to the Father is a journey. It takes time to move forward, step back, examine the work, trim the seams, and finish the stitches. The process of observing one's own life with the help of the Holy Spirit is to be aware of the disconnected places of our souls and finding the areas where the initial stitching may need to be corrected. As we read the Bible, He illuminates our hearts to truth. Hebrews 4:12 tells us, "The word of God is alive and active. Sharper than any double-edged sword, it penetrates even to dividing soul and spirit, joints and marrow; it judges the thoughts and attitudes of the heart."

The Word of God is the guide for the new person God is creating us to be. We must take the time to study it and allow the Holy Spirit to reveal to us the thoughts and attitudes within that are disconnected from His truth.

I make slipcovers because I love the work of creating beauty from nothing. I've often been asking if I would give up sewing to write. What I've realized is that I want to do the work, just like I want you to do the work of connecting to God in your own life. To have a heart filled with the peace of God, you have to want to be known and loved by Him. The desire must be stronger than the fear of His wrath or the fear of pruning.

This all circles back to our week about belief. God wants to create beauty from the pieces of your life. He will trim away the excess, remove some stitching, and sew again. It won't all feel pleasant. But He will create a masterpiece out of your life.

Read: Philippians 3:10-12, "I want to know Christ—yes, to know the power of his resurrection and participation in his sufferings, becoming like him in his death, and so, somehow, attaining to the resurrection from the dead. Not that I have already obtained all this, or have already arrived at my goal, but I press on to take hold of that for which Christ Jesus took hold of me."

Reflect: As you have worked through this week, has your desire to know Him grown? In what ways do you want to press toward knowing Him? (Think not necessarily what you can do physically, but also in terms of heart attitude.)

Record Your Thoughts

Prayer: Lord, I want to know You more. Help my heart to focus on the goal of knowing You and connecting with You throughout all the moments of my day. Amen.

Power Prayer for Week 11: Thank You for loving me unconditionally.

Week 12: Integrated Connection

Thank You for helping me to process stress in a creative and healthy way.

Day 1

After fitting the bodice, I moved to the full train of the ballroom wedding gown and draped the fabric, while I looked for the best solution for a flattering bustle. The mother of the bride queried how I gained such a talent, which led to a meandering conversation about sewing as a child and turning it into a business. I had a talent that I didn't know could be a profitable occupation.

The Bible reminds us we have all been given talents. One of the most well-known passages on talents is Matthew 25:14-30. I pondered this portion of Scripture as I wrote chapter 10 of my first book, "Beyond Head Knowledge: Knowing Christ Who Satisfies our Hearts." Recall the passage for a moment: The master went on a journey and left the first servant with five talents, the second two talents and the third one talent. The first two invested their talents, but the third buried his talent because he was afraid of the master.

I had spent much of my energy focused on searching for what I could do for God, and I was afraid I would waste my life. He showed me first I needed to consider what I was given to do. You guessed it—I realized that sewing was a talent with which He had entrusted me, and He was calling me to be faithful in that.[26] Faithfulness in sewing has often meant diligence in the work as well as being attentive to the client. Colossians 3:23 has become a foundational principle of business—that I would serve my clients as I would serve the Lord.

I don't know what talents you have been given. But we are all entrusted with one responsibility, and that is to care for our own souls. You've had a past. Perhaps it involved pain, trauma, or a dysfunctional family. We've all come from something. Though we can't change the past, we can work with God to process it, learn to know ourselves, and work to develop healthy relationships.

This process of working through the past will clear our souls of some of that cluttered anxiety and open alternative paths of deeper connection to God and to others.

Read: Matthew 25:29 (NLT), "To those who use well what they are given, even more will be given, and they will have an abundance. But from those who do nothing, even what little they have will be taken away."[27]

Reflect: Consider what you have been given, both from your past and in your current situation. List current responsibilities (family, kids, business, church). In what ways is God challenging you to be faithful with what you have been given?

Record Your Thoughts

Prayer: Thank You, Lord, for the talents with which You have entrusted me. I desire to be a good steward and to invest wisely in the responsibilities I have. I know that You will give me the strength and wisdom to do so. Amen.

Power Prayer for Week 12: Thank You for helping me to process stress in a creative and healthy way.

Day 2

As a writer, I will often join book launch teams to support other authors. I began reading "Busting Barriers" by Dr. Gladys Childs, for the book launch and I stopped at the sewing analogy. "Our relationships with colleagues, friends, or family are like intricate tapestries woven with threads of shared moments, challenges, and growth. We often believe that if love is genuine, it should flow effortlessly. But remember, even the most beautiful tapestries have knots and tangles on the underside. Those knots represent moments of struggle and compromise, the things that strengthen our bonds." [28]

As I read these words from Dr. Childs, I was reminded of how complicated relationships can be and how much the drama of them can affect our inner life of peace. There will be times of struggle as we navigate the complexities of all the relationships in our lives—times when we wrestle through a healthy response or wonder if we've done or said the wrong thing. There will be moments when words have come out of our mouth that caused pain to another and we will work to reconcile. Sometimes, it is the words or actions of others that hurt or offend us.

I think of my own marriage and parenting. There have been many times when I have spoken harsh or angry words. Though I have a wonderful relationship with my husband and children, it is far from perfect. We live in a fallen world. We are not perfect, and neither are others. The path of peace does not mean sweeping it all under the carpet to pretend hurt did not occur. Nor does it mean that we try to exert our own views on every relationship around us.

Perhaps we find peace by drawing close to the heart of God and talking to Him about the knots that have formed on the underside. Through this we become vulnerable to the work of the Holy Spirit as He molds our inner selves into a beautiful tapestry of grace. No matter the relational conflicts, we come to reflect the love of God, our Father, from the inside out. It is about His love flowing out and into our relationships in authenticity.

Read: Galatians 5:13, "You, my brothers and sisters, were called to be free. But do not use your freedom to indulge the flesh; rather, serve one another humbly in love."

Proverbs 15:1-2, "A gentle answer turns away wrath, but a harsh word stirs up anger. The tongue of the wise adorns knowledge, but the mouth of the fool gushes folly."

Reflect: Name some challenging relationships in your life. Why are these relationships challenging? (There may be a different reason for each relationship.) Invite the Holy Spirit to reveal the hurt that you may have experienced in this area.

Record Your Thoughts

Prayer: Father, thank You for the relationships in my life, even those that are complicated. Thank You for using these relationships to propel me toward You and for causing me to grow more like You. I ask for wisdom and grace in each challenging relationship. Amen.

Power Prayer for Week 12: Thank You for helping me to process stress in a creative and healthy way.

Day 3

As terror over the COVID-19 pandemic and ensuing lockdown consumed the world, so did the panic over the PPE (personal protective equipment) shortage. In most parts of the United States, face masks became required in every public place, but the demand outpaced the supply. For sewists, this was a time to rise. I quickly gathered a team of sewists and volunteers in a mask making campaign that far outpaced my wildest dreams. Within days, I had a team of over 40 volunteers sewing, cutting, and delivering.[29] By the time the PPE shortage subsided, this team produced thousands of masks for businesses and first responders.

Fear and anxiety were a big part of the COVID pandemic. This was in part because of the fear of the disease itself. However, the social isolation of the pandemic had a significant impact on mental health[30] because we were made for connection. Lack of connection equals a lack of peace, which equates to anxiety and poor mental health.

During the pandemic, I'm thankful for the benefits of technology such as Zoom that helped me stay connected to friends, family, and business groups. Yet, the online connection can never replace being in someone's presence, such as when sitting across the table over a cup of coffee and looking into someone's eyes. We need interpersonal relationships to feel fully alive. There is no substitute for this.

When I sense a restless anxiety within my soul, I take account of my own relationships. I reflect on whether I have intentionally connected in person with healthy friendships over the past weeks. If this is lacking, I pray about ways to make time for real friends in real life.

If you struggle to make time for friends, here are some ideas:

- Purposefully connect with existing friends by meeting for coffee or regular phone chats.

- Join a community book club, or volunteer activity.

- Attend small groups at church.

- Invite a neighbor over for a cup of tea or light meal.

Find those relationships that enliven your soul and continue to invest in them on purpose.

Read: Proverbs 27:17, "As iron sharpens iron, so one person sharpens another."

Ecclesiastes 4:9-10, "Two are better than one, because they have a good return for their labor: If either of them falls down, one can help the other up. But pity anyone who falls and has no one to help them up."

Reflect: Do your friends build you up? If you are experiencing social isolation, what activities are available to you to build friendships?

Record Your Thoughts

Prayer: Lord, I know that social isolation is not good for my peace. Help me purposefully create opportunities to grow friendship by reaching outside my comfort zone. Amen.

Power Prayer for Week 12: Thank You for helping me to process stress in a creative and healthy way.

Day 4

In the days leading up to the launch of my first book, my two best friends from Bible college came to visit for a few days so they could attend the ladies' brunch hosted by my church as part of the book launch. Launching a book brings about a range of emotional highs and lows. I remember one of them commenting that if they didn't know where to find me, be sure to check the sewing room. They realized what I did not: sewing is a form of emotional therapy for me, even if it is just sewing for other people.

As we go through life, it is important to know yourself. Learn to connect with who you are, where you came from, and where you are going. Learn to manage your stress healthily and find activities that feed your soul. Recognize your strengths and weaknesses in your own schedule and observe the times you feel at peace and when you do not.

This leads to a more integrated and connected self as you learn to pay attention to the unique individual God created you to be and you lean into those strengths. Rather than pushing down feelings of emptiness or underlying anxiety, ask yourself what fills you and what activities rejuvenate your soul. Observe what those closest to you tell you about yourself. Often others see in us what we do not recognize in ourselves, just like it took my friends to tell me that sewing was stress relief.

This is a journey of discovery. As you connect with God in vulnerability, He will show you who He created you to be.

There are many things I realized over the years. For example, books fill my soul, but with my present responsibility I don't get many chances to read. Instead, I've realized that I am an audio processor, and listening to books while I'm sewing activates my mind and renews me. I've also learned that writing in the evening doesn't work, but sewing in the evening with an audiobook is golden.

Learn to know yourself: What speaks to you? What moves your soul? Pay attention to the unique individual God created you to be and lean into it.

Read: Psalm 139:2-4, "You know when I sit and when I rise; you perceive my thoughts from afar. You discern my going out and my lying down; you are familiar with all my ways. Before a word is on my tongue you, Lord, know it completely."

Reflect: God knows you and knows how He created you to deal with your stress. Where do you go or what do you do when you feel stressed? Is this a healthy activity? If not, what activity fills you and how can you make this your stress relief?

Record Your Thoughts

Prayer: Thank You, Lord, that You created me with creative outlets to help me process the tension in my life and body. Show me the unique and healthy ways that I can work out the internal stress I carry. Amen.

Power Prayer for Week 12: Thank You for helping me to process stress in a creative and healthy way.

Day 5

I woke with a start, having overslept the 5:00 a.m. alarm. A stiffening tension coursed throughout my entire body. I should have recognized the warning signs the day before as I compulsively checked my email every 30 minutes, looking for response emails from several clients. Dresses and deadlines filled my dreams as I carried the pressure within my soul.

Yet the invitation to the weary soul is to come and lay it down, trusting that He holds it all in His hands. But when the demands of this life feel so real, how can we learn to accept that invitation? I quickly forget that He is faithful. He was faithful so many times throughout my story.

With new situations, I must learn to stitch the connection from his past faithfulness to belief and reliance on His current faithfulness. The promise of rest fills Hebrews 4. This is the invitation—rest for our souls is available. We don't have to live striving in the activities of life and business. Instead, He says the promise of rest is still ours for the taking. Strong's concordance comments on the Greek root of rest and states, "God's rest is entered when the believer is confidently assured within and outwardly lives peaceably in the assurance of God's daily provision."[31]

Rest in Him is a mystery. We cannot see the mystery of resting in Him, but we can feel it in our bodies as we confidently trust in God. When I am not experiencing His rest, I feel the tension of burdens I have been trying to carry myself. I must take deliberate actions to lay these down again. This is surrender. I surrender my control of the burden because I trust. Perhaps the golden thread of the Christian life is this surrender.

In most cases surrender involves letting go of what we are holding onto or defending. I've learned that surrender also means letting go of my fears. When the deadlines mount, I feel the tension because I'm afraid that I will not meet the deadline. I must learn to turn these fears over to God by telling Him, "I'm feeling overwhelmed by the work, I know that You can orchestrate my time in such a way that I have the time to do what needs to be done. I believe that You will guide my hands with each stitch." This helps me let go of my fears and confesses belief in God's ability.

Rather than holding on, let go and trust Him.

Read: Hebrews 4:1-2, "Therefore, since the promise of entering his rest still stands, let us be careful that none of you be found to have fallen short of it. For we also have had the good news proclaimed to us, just as they did; but the message they heard was of no value to them, because they did not share the faith of those who obeyed."

Reflect: Do you feel tension in your body? How do you know? What is the root of it?

Record Your Thoughts

Prayer: Lord, I come to you with these stressors: _____. You have been faithful in the past and I believe You are faithful now. I lay them down. Help me enter into Your rest. Amen.

Power Prayer for Week 12: Thank You for helping me to process stress in a creative and healthy way.

Day 6

My daughter sat at the machine to sew the knit hem lining of a prom dress. She put the presser foot down and stitched. The needle moved up and down as the upper thread connected to the bobbin, forming stitches. However, the fabric didn't move. The stitches piled on top of each other until there was a big knot on the underside. The fabric had been forcefully pulled below the throat plate, and it required removing the plate and carefully removing the stitches to untangle it.

Here, the problem started because the edge had caught in the feed dogs with the first stitches. Jams like this often take place when we are in a hurry or aren't paying attention. As you have been working through the connections and relationships in your life, you may rush to fix them all at once. Frequently, this can create a bigger mess because you simply cannot process or fix everything at once.

If you have found yourself stuck while on this journey of connection, slow down and look for the stuck places. Pray. Seek wise council. Find silence and allow the Holy Spirit to shine a light on what only He can.

Shortly after my dad (Walt) passed, I was in a stuck place as grief consumed me and God seemed far away. I struggled to connect with God even though I was crying out to Him. That fall, a Christian family from Ghana moved to our development. Our kids were friends which led me to invite the mother over as well. She was fascinated by my sewing business and since she was not working at the time, I invited her to join me in sewing during the week. This blossomed into a beautiful friendship. For the next year we enjoyed laughter and fellowship over the needles and thread. It was healing for my grief and helped me restore connection with God the Father and with others.

When we seek Him, He will help us when we are stuck. Just like He provided a friend to sew with me in my time of need, He can also provide what you need to restore connection. This was not a solution that took place in 24 hours. It was a year of relationship that grew slowly. No matter what season you feel stuck in, God will answer in ways you least expect. Don't give up or lose hope. This is all part of stitching.

Read: Galatians 6:9, "Let us not become weary in doing good, for at the proper time we will reap a harvest if we do not give up."

1 Timothy 6:19-20, "Command them to do good, to be rich in good deeds, and to be generous and willing to share. In this way they will lay up

treasure for themselves as a firm foundation for the coming age, so that they may take hold of the life that is truly life."

Reflect: Have you been weary in the work of building healthy relationships? What is the promise of these Scriptures? How do they give you hope?

Record Your Thoughts

Prayer: Lord, Thank You from the promise of harvest and a firm foundation. I receive the strength You give to continue on in building healthy relationships. Thank You for wisdom and discernment as well. Amen.

Power Prayer for Week 12: Thank You for giving me wisdom to build healthy relationships.

Week 13: Choose Your Stitches

Thank You for empowering me to choose the path of peace, which is life to me and my descendants after me.

Day 1

By the early 1900s, the garment district of New York City comprised 46% of the city's industrial labor.[32] It's no wonder that so many of my clients tell me their grandmothers worked in factories! Living only a few hours from the city, many families in my area migrated from New York City in past generations.

One client told the story of her grandmother who sewed at a garment factory. A handsome young man also worked at the factory as a sewing machine repair technician. Determined to make his acquaintance, she aided a breakdown of her sewing machine just so she could meet him. Not to give up easily, she continued to need sewing machine repairs. Her persistence paid off and some time later, they were married.

Persistence is a key factor in a peaceful life. In Ephesians, Paul encourages us to be strong in the Lord and fight the battle. My journey toward peace did not come without persistence. Some days when I have felt consumed by fear, all the toxic thoughts run circles in my head. It's all I can do to breathe the prayers,

"Lord, I believe that You have not given me a spirit of fear, but of love, power and a sound mind."

"Lord, I believe that because I am Your child, You have given me the mind of Christ."

I believe. The words of Scripture are my sword. I am determined. Fear and anxiety are not our lot in life. With perseverance, you can fight the fear and anxiety that you experience. This devotional has predominantly focused using Scripture and the word of God. There are also valuable resources available to us in the form of medical help, counseling, or dietary changes. If you need some of these other resources to fight the battle, please seek them out.

The prophet Isaiah believed God promised His people peace and wrote, "You will keep in perfect peace those whose minds are steadfast, because they trust in you (Isaiah 26:3)." Persist in trusting God and the promised peace will be yours.

Read: Ephesians 6:10-13, "Finally, be strong in the Lord and in his mighty power. Put on the full armor of God, so that you can take your stand against the devil's schemes. For our struggle is not against flesh and blood, but against the rulers, against the authorities, against the powers of this dark world and against the spiritual forces of evil in the heavenly realms. Therefore put on the full armor of God, so that when the day of evil comes, you may be able to stand your ground, and after you have done everything, to stand."

Reflect: When did you need to persist for what you wanted? Will you persistently fight for peace?

Record Your Thoughts

Prayer: Lord, thank You for the armor of God. I will put on my armor and fight the battle with Your strength. I will not give up because I know that peace is Your will for me. Amen.

Power Prayer for Week 13: Thank You for empowering me to choose the path of peace, which is life to me and my descendants after me.

Day 2

My daughter sat at the serger, finishing the edges of a cushion cover. I was around the corner in my office. A sound from the machine caught my attention. It was the sound the machine makes when it is going over a bulky area and protesting. I've had this machine for 15 years, and over that length of time I've learned to recognize its "voice" from the sounds it makes. Currently it was protesting the speed at which my daughter was trying to go over the tough parts. I paused the bookkeeping at my desk to demonstrate how to handle the machine over the thick joining seams.

Every sewing machine has its own voice. Through consistent time spent with a machine, you will learn to recognize what the sounds mean, if you pay attention.

God has a voice. In my first book, "Beyond Head Knowledge," I write about learning to recognize the voice of the Holy Spirit. I write of the years I struggled with guilt because "I confused the voice of the Holy Spirit with my own overactive conscience." [33] There were also times that I was extremely confused about the will of God because I would hear all sorts of contradicting voices in my head.

Throughout history many have been confused about the voice of God. Once there was a boy named Samuel, who served in the temple. One night he heard a voice. He thought it was his temple mentor, Eli. But Eli told him it was not and sent him back to bed. This happened three times, until Eli told Samuel that the voice must be the voice of God. The next time Samuel heard the voice, he responded to God, "Speak, Lord, your servant is listening." (1 Samuel 3)

Inability to recognize the voice of God leads to anxiety and confusion. Jesus clearly teaches that as Christians, we need to learn to know His voice. In John 10, He gives the illustration of sheep who know the voice of their shepherd. He is able to lead them to safety because they know His voice and follow Him. As you develop a deeper connection with God, you will begin to recognize the way He speaks to you.

Read: John 10:3b-5, "He calls his own sheep by name and leads them out. When he has brought out all his own, he goes on ahead of them, and his sheep follow him because they know his voice. But they will never follow a stranger; in fact, they will run away from him because they do not recognize a stranger's voice."

Reflect: Have you ever clearly heard God speaking to you? Do you feel confused about the voice of God?

Record Your Thoughts

Prayer: Father, I want to recognize your voice. Tune my ears to listen and understand. I believe it is Your will that I hear Your voice directing my steps. Amen.

Power Prayer for Week 13: Thank You for empowering me to choose the path of peace, which is life to me and my descendants after me.

Day 3

As usual, I awoke with a long to-do list. My top priority was to finish a wing chair slipcover. But the day didn't go according to plan. During my two-to-three-hour window, in the afternoon while the kids napped, a friend called who needed prayer. One thing led to another, and I knew that God was directing my afternoon, but it wasn't what I had planned.

I used to internally freak out about such divine interruptions. Sometimes I covered my ears to the quiet nudging of the Holy Spirit, telling Him that I had deadlines and just didn't have time for His plans.

This is the quandary: sometimes in the pursuit of peace God also disturbs our peace. Obedience to the promptings of the Holy Spirit can feel like stress. The trust you have built over the past 13 weeks comes in here. Do you believe that God is telling you to do something? Do you believe that He will work out the to-do list if you obey? Do you believe that God's plan for you is better than your own?

Actions and belief need to work together to align in our souls. Being a Christian means that you believe God will lead you and guide you. If you truly believe the Bible, you believe that following or obeying Him is the path to life (and peace). Yet still your natural reasoning will war against the directions God is giving you.

After dinner, I sat down at the sewing machine. I was hours behind because of the missed afternoon sewing. The hours passed. As bedtime neared, I marveled at the goodness of God. What should have taken me six hours to complete only took three.

Throughout the years I have seen this pan out many times. Though I am diligent to plan a schedule for the week, God's direction must take top priority. My dad used to say it like this: Available + Prepared + Expectant = Opportunity. When we are available, prepared and expectant for God to show up in our everyday lives, He will show up with opportunity to follow and obey.

Read: Isaiah 55:8-9, "'For my thoughts are not your thoughts, neither are your ways my ways,' declares the LORD. 'As the heavens are higher than the earth, so are my ways higher than your ways and my thoughts than your thoughts.'"

Reflect: Have you ever felt God was interrupting your plans? What was your response? What do you want your response to be in the future?

Record Your Thoughts

Prayer: Lord, I believe that my purpose on earth is to bring glory to You. Sometimes listening to Your thoughts about what I should do is very different from what I had already planned. I repent for the times I have elevated the importance of my plan over Your plan. Help me to listen and obey, believing that You will work out my to-do list in Your own way. Amen.

Power Prayer for Week 13: Thank You for empowering me to choose the path of peace, which is life to me and my descendants after me.

Day 4

Good Friday was a quiet day in the sewing room. I decided this was an opportunity to clean the machines. The past few weeks had been busy between slipcovers and wedding gowns. My serger still had a lot of brown fibers laying in the feed dogs and gears. As I dismantled the machines, taking off the throat plates, dusting and oiling as needed, I moved the handwheel to adjust the needle position.

Down went the needle. The picture before my eyes – He was buried. As He went down into the ground from sight. Up came the needle. He is risen. As He rose a secure stitch formed. As we enter in, the death, burial and resurrection of Christ stitches us to the Father. This is the picture of His perfect love. I am stitched to Him, with a stitch that can't be broken.

This mystery is only available when we submit ourselves to being hidden. Colossians 3:3 reminds us that when we come to Christ, we die. We are hidden with Christ in God. Dead to fear. Dead to our natural thinking of planning and controlling. Dead to exalting our knowledge over His.

This journey towards peace has been one of death. My thoughts and actions had been dictated by my perception of my past and present, which in turn caused great worry about the future. Because He died and rose again, we do not need to live according to what we see with our eyes. The words of Galatians 2, "My old self has been crucified with Christ. It is no longer I who live but Christ lives in me. So I live in this earthly body by trusting in the Son of God, who loved me and gave Himself for me (NLT)." We die to all those thoughts and attitudes so that we He comes alive in us. This all happens by learning to trust Him with all moments of our life, which includes health, family, travel, plans, schedules and so much more. We die to our projection of the outcome and to our control over our schedules and ask for divine wisdom—for the presence and person of Christ to penetrate all of life.

This is the motion of the needle. Down—we submit our thoughts. Up—we come up with His truth on our lips and filling our minds. The stitch is formed strengthening our connection of trust with the Father.

Peace comes as we let the full weight of His Life consume us in His love. You are loved. Hidden in His embrace. It is safe. Relax. Let go. Die so you can live.

Read: Colossians 3:3, "For you died, and your life is now hidden with Christ in God."

Reflect: How have you died to your old way of thinking through the past three months?

Record Your Thoughts

Prayer: Father, as I take on the identity of being hidden in Christ, I have found new life. Thank You for transforming me from the inside out to walk the path of peace. Amen.

Power Prayer for Week 13: Thank You for empowering me to choose the path of peace, which is life to me and my descendants after me.

Day 5

For wedding gowns, I prefer an 8- to 10-week lead time. This gives enough time to do the alterations without feeling rushed and allows for several fittings. One winter, a bride contacted me months before her wedding, saying her gown wouldn't be arriving until three weeks before the ceremony, asking if I could give her an appointment now to hold an alteration spot for when the dress arrived.

Months later, I arrived at her home for the fitting. Her gown had arrived the day before, but to her dismay it was not what she expected. It was lace with white lining—however, the white lining was only under the skirt, because the bodice was made of mesh. This meant the nude skin color showed through the bodice, but the waistline was an eyesore as the stark contrast of white and nude was exacerbated. She hoped it would be possible to change the lining to nude.

With a slim timeline, I went to work sourcing fabric for the lining, and said a few prayers as I detached the entire skirt from the bodice and zipper. Days later, the work was finished. As I arranged the gown on the dress form to design the bustle, I forced myself to pause. Even though the work was not fully complete, I gave thanks for the work of beauty in front of me. I knew there were some slight imperfections. For example, the lining was not as good quality as I hoped and already had several pills in it.

I used to rush from project to project, hardly giving time to marvel and celebrate the completion of one. This formed a spirit of striving. God was also a creative. He formed the world in six days with His voice. Each day, even when He was not yet finished, He stepped back and said, "It is good."

I don't always pause to give thanks, proclaiming that it is good. You've begun your journey toward peace and are making progress. Pause to give thanks. The work God is doing in you is good. Don't get fixated on how far you have left to go. Celebrate the small victories.

Read: Isaiah 26:3-4, "You will keep in perfect peace those whose minds are steadfast, because they trust in you. Trust in the Lord forever, for the Lord, the Lord himself, is the Rock eternal."

Reflect: Write some specific examples of progress you have seen over the past 12 weeks. No example is too small. Pause to thank God. Make a habit of reflecting on the faithfulness of God, and from where He has brought you. This will grow your faith.

Record Your Thoughts

Prayer: Father, thank You for the work You are doing in me. I know You will continue to work on me for the rest of my life. Help me continue to draw close to You and remain teachable. Amen.

Power Prayer for Week 13: Thank You for empowering me to choose the path of peace, which is life to me and my descendants after me.

Day 6

The summer before I got married, I was a bridesmaid in my best friend's wedding. A homeschool friend who operated a sewing business from her home was making the gowns. Since she lived on the west coast of the United States and I on the east coast I sent her my body measurements for the dress but didn't get to try it on until days before the wedding. A seed of hope was born, as I walked into the home sewing studio to pick up my dress. I sewed. Perhaps someday I too could work from home to be present with my children.

Over the next year that seed of hope took root and grew. I told my dad, Walt, and my fiancé this was something I thought I could do. Dad set my hope into motion by naming my business and printing my first business cards. From there the work was up to me. I needed to register as a DBA with the county, set up a business bank account, professionally answer the phone and much more.

Through this book I pray I have planted a seed of hope—hope that you too can pursue a life of peace, rather than fear and anxiety. However, I can't do all the work for you. Through my story you see it's possible. It's available and peace is God's gift to you.

I had a creative interest in sewing, coupled with the desire to be home with my kids. God took these desires and built something beautiful. It didn't happen all at once, rather over the course of several years it was one decision after another that led to where I am today. The days are not easy, but I experience great joy as I reap the fruit of the endeavor. The choice to run a sewing business has changed the course of my life and that of my family. Rather than living the years feeling stuck because of the circumstances of the past God led me into the desires of my heart.

He longs to do the same for you. He created you with unique desires and talents. Every day God puts choices before you, both big and small. Learn to pause listening to the voice of your Good Father. He wants to lead you in a path of peace as you trust Him for all things in life. Peace doesn't mean that you get everything you want, it means leaning on Him to direct your steps, being brave enough to do the hard things He is showing you and trusting that He is good. The choice is yours. I have laid before you life and death, what will you choose? Your choice stitches your story.

Read: Deuteronomy 30:19, "This day I call the heavens and the earth as witnesses against you that I have set before you life and death, blessings and curses. Now choose life, so that you and your children may live."

Reflect: As you look back over the past 13 weeks, write down changes that you see in your thoughts, actions, and beliefs. These changes are life. Will you choose life today, tomorrow and for the rest of your life?

Record Your Thoughts

Prayer: Father, thank You for Your great love that stitches my life securely to You. I choose life. I believe through the power of Your Spirit, You will be faithful to lead me on the path of peace, which is life. Amen.

Power Prayer for Week 13: Thank You for empowering me to choose the path of peace, which is life to me and my descendants after me.

Epilogue

As you move forward in peace, remember that the most important thing is spending time with Your Father. He is the author of peace. There is no substitute for daily time with Him through stillness, Bible reading, and prayer. Your relationship with Him is the most important thing in your life. The weeks that you have spent processing and journaling with me here are not meant to be the end, but the beginning of a lifelong pursuit of peace.

Acknowledgements

My husband Tony for being my biggest cheerleader. Thank you for always believing in me and in the work God has called me to do.

Malachi, Aryana, and Gianni, who gave me the uninterrupted 40 minutes a day to write.

My mom, who homeschooled the kids one day a week for several years so I could have uninterrupted participation in the Inkwell writing group.

My long-time friends Anna Ahrens and Karen Skinner for their support and encouragement through all my book crazy.

Barb Zelie, thank you for reading and offering your feedback. I know you think it was insignificant, but it was far more meaningful than you can imagine.

Sue McCormick, Beth Cooper, Jeanann Schneider, and Bonnie Drowne who also read excerpts and offered valuable feedback.

Rosemary Keener, for the intercessory prayer she has prayed over me and the writing during our weekly prayer time.

Dalene Bickel and the Inkwell Community, for the weekly writing time, friendship, prayer, and community. I would not have finished writing without you.

Melissa Lennie, my newfound sewing sister, who loves Jesus and sewing as much as I do.

Christa Hutchins and the Honor Circle, who cheered me along in the process.

Ruthie Gray and her communities, who first birthed the idea of writing about faith from the voice of a sewist.

Julie Cicora, author of "Contemplative Knitting," encouraged me with the possibilities of writing with sewing.

Terry Grahl, founder of Enchanted Makeovers, thank you for reminding me to serve with my talents.

To every client and friend who may be reflected in these stories. Thank you for telling your story.

Christian Resource Ministry board, thank you for believing in this project.

Sarah Geringer for her dedication and hard work in editing and formatting this manuscript.

Glossary

Foot Pedal: Most sewing machines are operated with your foot, using a small pedal on the floor, which has a cord plugging into the sewing machine.

Hem (verb): To shorten an item of clothing such as a pair of pants, shirt, or gown, and to finish the edge with a seam.

Raw Edge: An edge of fabric that is not sewn, which often means it will fray.

Serger: a type of sewing machine used for overcasting, also called over-locking, which prevents material from fraying at the edge.

Throat Plate: Metal piece under the needle and presser foot. It is usually held in place by several screws.

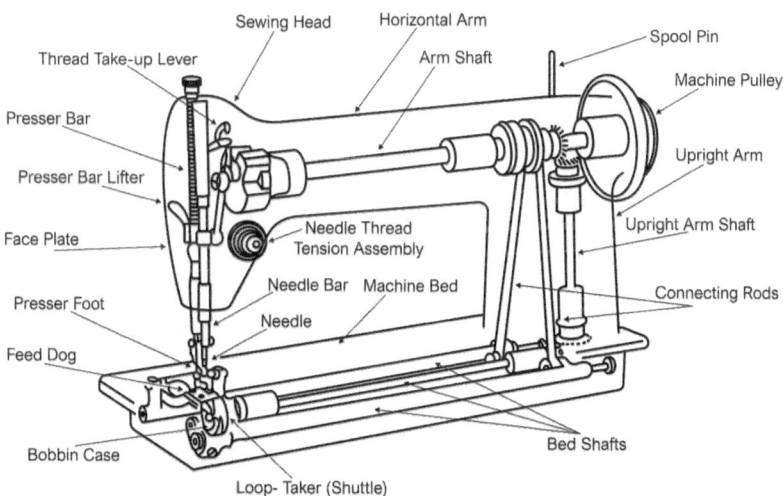

Recommended Reading

The books on this list deeply impacted my journey and you may notice some of the ideas these authors present reflected in my writing. This is not an exhaustive list.

Clinton, Dr. Tim and Straub, Dr. Joshua
   "God Attachment: Why You Believe, Act, and Feel the Way You Do About God"
Cloud, Dr. Henry & Dr. John Townsend
   "Boundaries: When to Say Yes, How to Say No, to Take Control of Your Life"
   "It's Not My Fault: The No-Excuse Plan to Put You in Charge of Your Life"
Crabb, Larry
   "Connecting: Healing for Ourselves and Our Relationships"
Dalton-Smith MD, Sandra
   "Sacred Rest: Recover Your Life, Renew Your Energy, Restore Your Sanity"
Jennings, Dr. Timothy
   "Could It Be This Simple: A Biblical Model for Healing the Mind"
   "The God-Shaped Brain: How Changing Your View of God Transforms Your Life"
   "The God-Shaped Heart: How Correctly Understanding God's Love Transforms Us"
Johnson, Bill
   "The Supernatural Power of a Transformed Mind: Access to a Life of Miracles"
Leaf, Dr. Caroline
   "Who Switched Off My Brain? Controlling Toxic Thoughts and Emotions"
   "Switch on My Brain: The Key to Peak Happiness, Thinking and Health"
Meyer, Joyce
   "Power Thoughts: 12 Strategies to Win the Battle of the Mind"
Ortberg, John
   "Soul Keeping: Caring for the Most Important Part of You"
Schneider, K. A.
   "Self-Deliverance: How to Gain Victory Over the Powers of Darkness"
Schuller, Bobby
   "Happiness According to Jesus: What it Means to be Blessed"

Thompson M.D., Curt
    "Anatomy of the Soul: Surprising Connection Between Neuroscience and Spiritual Practices that Can Transform Your Life and Relation-ships"
Welch, Edward T.
    "Depression: Looking Up from the Stubborn Darkness"
Willard, Dallas
    "Divine Conspiracy: Rediscovering Our Hidden Life in God"

About the Author

Naomi Fata is a professional sewist specializing in bridal alterations and custom fitted slipcovers. In her spare time, she is a speaker, author, and regular contributor to God's Corner for her local newspaper. Naomi has earned certificates and degrees in the following areas: Christian life coaching, Bible, psychology, non-profit management and social welfare. She and her husband Tony live in upstate New York and homeschool their three children.

Instagram: @naomifata
Facebook: @naomifatasews
YouTube: @naomifatasews
Sign up for a monthly ministry newsletter at
www.christianresourceministry.com
or her sewing newsletter at www.naomifata.net.

Endnotes

1   Cullum, Amber, host. "Leigh Mackenzie: The Value of Trauma Therapy & Journaling with Jesus." Grace Enough Podcast. Episode 215 https://www.graceenoughpodcast.com/trauma/ Retrieved March 29, 2024.

2   Cline, Elizabeth L. "Overdressed: The Shockingly High Cost of Cheap Fashion." London, Penguin Books, 2012, p. 90.

3   Clinton, Dr. Tim and Straub, Dr. Joshua. "God Attachment: Why You Believe, Act, and Feel the Way You Do About God." New York, Howard Books, 2010, p. 52.

4   Morris, Henry. "The Henry Morris Study Bible, King James Version." Green Forest, Arizona, Masterbooks, 2012, p. 1824.

5   Brandom, Chad; Draper, Charles; and England, Archie. "Holman Illustrated Bible Dictionary." Nashville, Holman Bible Publishers, 2003. P. 1430.

6   Reimann, Jim. "Look Unto Me: The Devotions of Charles Spurgeon." Grand Rapids, Zondervan, 2008, p. 333.

7   Willard, Dallas. "The Divine Conspiracy: Rediscovering Our Hidden Life in God." San Fransisco, Harper San Francisco, 1997, pp. 55-57.

8   Mazzella, Randi. "How Helping Others Helps You." Psycom. May, 30, 2023. https://www.psycom.net/mental-health-wellbeing/how-helping-others-improves-mental-health Retrieved November 1, 2023.

9   Strong, James. "Rest." Strong's Expanded Exhaustive Concordance of the Bible. Nashville: Thomas Nelson, 2001.

10   Hunter, Claire. "Threads of Life: History of the World Through the Eye of a Needle." New York, Abrams Press, 2019. Ebook, p. 412.

11   Strong, James. ibid.

12   Hunter, Claire. ibid.

13   Webster, Noah. "1828 Wester's Dictionary." https://webstersdictionary1828.com/Dictionary/faith Retrieved November 17, 2023.

14   Ortberg, John. "Soul Keeping: Caring for the Most Important Part of You." Grand Rapids, Zondervan, 2014. Electronic version.

15   Henry, Matthew. "Matthew Henry's Commentary Matthew to John." MacDonald Publishing Company. McLean, Virginia, 1985, p. 326.

16   Leaf, Dr. Caroline. "Who Switched Off My Brain? Controlling Toxic Thoughts and Emotions." Switch on Your Brain, South Africa, 2007, p. 35.

17   Jennings, Timothy M.D. "The God Shaped Brain: How Changing Your View of God Transforms Your Life." InterVarsity Press, Downers Grove, IL, 2013, p. 63.

18   Leaf, Dr. Caroline. Ibid, p. 109.

19   Jennings, Timothy M.D., Ibid, p. 63.

20   Voskamp, Ann. "One Thousand Gifts: A Dare to Live Fully Right Where You Are." Grand Rapids, Michigan, Zondervan, 2010.

21   C.S. Lewis, "Mere Christianity." New York, Touchstone, a division of Simon & Schuster, 1996, p. 190.

22   Edwards, Zoe, host. "How to care for your sewing machine with Bizz McKilligan." Check Your Thread, episode 120, January 22, 2024. Accessed May 29. 2024.

23   Crabb, Larry. "Connecting: Healing for Ourselves and our Relationships A Radical New Vision." E-book ed. W Publishing Group, 1997.

24   Jennings, Timothy M.D., Ibid, p. 38.

25   Edwards, Jada. "When You Pray: A Study of Six Prayers in the Bible." Brentwood, TN, LifeWay Press, 2023.

26   Fata, Naomi. "Beyond Head Knowledge: Knowing Christ Who Satisfies Our Hearts." Greenville, Ambassador International, 2014, p. 135.

27   Holy Bible, New Living Translation, Tyndale Charitable Trust, 1996, 2004

28   Childs, Dr. Gladys. "Busting Barriers: Overcome Emptiness and Unleash Fruitful Living." Self-published, 2023, p. 9.

29   "Red Hook woman leads sewing initiative that's created 1,200 masks since March 21." The Daily Freemen, Kingston, NY, April 15, 2020. https://www.dailyfreeman.com/2020/04/15/red-hook-woman-leads-sewing-initiative-thats-created-1200-masks-since-march-21/ Accessed May 10, 2024.

30   Jeffers, Alexiss, Ashley A. Meehan, Jordan Barker, Alice Asher, Martha P. Montgomery, Greg Bautista, Colleen M. Ray, Rebecca L. Laws, Victoria L. Fields, Lakshmi Radhakrishnan, and et al. 2022. "Impact of Social Isolation during the COVID-19 Pandemic on Mental Health, Substance Use, and Homelessness: Qualitative Interviews with Behavioral Health Providers." International Journal of Environmental Research and Public Health no. 19: 12120. https://doi.org/10.3390/ijerph191912120

31   Strong, James. "Rest." Strong's Expanded Exhaustive Concordance of the Bible. Nashville: Thomas Nelson, 2001.

32   Montero, Gabriel. "A Stitch in Time: A History of New York's Fashion District." https://garmentdistrict.nyc/history. Retrieved March 29, 2024.

33   Fata, Naomi. ibid.

www.ingramcontent.com/pod-product-compliance
Lightning Source LLC
Chambersburg PA
CBHW020239130626
46549CB00005B/1972